D0984475

CONTEMPLATIVE
CHRISTIANITY

Contemplative Christianity

AN APPROACH TO THE REALITIES OF RELIGION

AELRED GRAHAM

'*I am constantly moved by the question what Christianity
really is, or who Christ really is, for us today*'
                                        Dietrich Bonhoeffer

A CROSSROAD BOOK
THE SEABURY PRESS • NEW YORK

The Seabury Press
815 Second Avenue
New York, N.Y. 10017

LIBRARY OF CONGRESS CATALOGING IN PUBLICATION DATA

Graham, Aelred, 1907-
    Contemplative Christianity.
    "A Crossroad book."
    Includes index.
    1. Spiritual life.   2. Christianity—20th century.
3. Christianity and other religions.   I. Title.
BV4501.2.G724   1975   248′.3   74-26989
ISBN 0-8164-0269-8

for
E.P.M.

Preface

THE APPENDIX to this essay could usefully be read first. An enterprising publisher noticed it in its original form as an article in *The Times* of London and invited me to expand it into a book. The seven chapters which follow are the result of this suggestion. They might well have been entitled 'Themes for a changing Church', though that would imply too narrow a focus. They amount to a series of observations about Christianity—counterpointed with Eastern religion, especially Buddhism—addressed to anyone who finds these topics interesting and is prepared to reflect on them. They are more likely to evoke a sympathetic response from the younger, or at least more open-minded generation, than from those who have long-settled views on these questions.

The word 'contemplative' is used in a double sense. First, as applied to a state of mind—possible, I think, for a Christian as well as others—in which he or she looks calmly and without prejudice at the institutional Church, as a truth-seeker, and therefore neither defensive nor hostile, concerned merely to discover how things are. Secondly, 'contemplative' applies to the individual's spiritual life. The aim is to lead the mind, so far as this can be done by the use of words, from signs and symbols to the realities they signify. It is here that Indian religion has much to offer. Without confusing the two, we shall attempt to show in passing how much Christianity and the Hindu-Buddhist tradition have in common, at least potentially. More urgently needed than programmes for Church renewal, it seems to me, is an honest facing up to the assumptions that underlie the generally accepted Christian proclamation. This means examining some of the critical questions which are normally evaded at ecumenical discussions.

The days of the elaborate theological syntheses are over. The foundations on which they could be built are no longer there. Instead, the more pressing requirement lies in the direction of what might be called, somewhat portentously, prolegomena to any future presentation of Christianity. Or more simply, what the scholastics used to designate the *status quaestionis*: that is to say, a comprehensive analysis of the preliminaries indispensable to any useful discussion about the place of the Church in the life of humanity as a whole. Meanwhile, pending the arrival on the scene of minds with the necessary competence to undertake the task, an unpretentious sketch or two may be in order. A few seeds of thought (to change the metaphor) are here being dropped for the benefit of those who might find them worthwhile—by one whose chief qualification (not by any means the highest) lies in the probability that he has been able to observe rather more of the world's religious phenomena, and been given longer time to think about them, than falls to the lot of the average theoretician of the spiritual life. There could be a little matter here for churchmen and theologians to take note of; but the essay is intended for the reflective general reader, particularly among the rising generation and those who feel some responsibility for them.

Ampleforth Abbey   AELRED GRAHAM
York

Contents

CONTEMPLATIVE
CHRISTIANITY

1   The widening of the options

'AT THE present moment there are two things about the Christian religion which must be obvious to every percipient person,' observed Matthew Arnold in the reign of Queen Victoria. 'One, that men cannot do without it; the other that they cannot do with it as it is.' That was a century ago. Today even the most unperceptive churchman may concede that there is something wrong with Christianity as it is. But now we are obliged to go further and admit that there are plenty of people who can do without it altogether. This was true of the Victorian age, as Arnold would doubtless have agreed; for our contemporaries it has become a truism. Apart from the hundreds of millions in Asia who have always done without it, Christianity as a religion for the western world has begun to present itself as but one option among many.

The means hardly exist for examining this situation statistically. Head counting, in terms of baptisms, communicants and attendance at church, gives little indication of what is really going on inside people's minds. Many of the Christian churches, by virtue of their holdings in real estate, constitute enormous vested interests—for which self-preservation takes high priority. Church officials, with few exceptions, see themselves as committed upholders of an historic tradition, not as concerned expositors of religious truth in the light of all the available evidence. However inevitable this state of affairs may be, given that signs of stability are commonly looked for in religion as elsewhere, it helps to explain why in a changing and revolutionary world, the Church's message, while still resolutely proclaimed, is increasingly losing its appeal.

At its beginnings Christianity had about it a sense of urgency; it was a life and death affair; it really mattered whether you believed or not. Even when the early apocalyptic expectations of some brave new world remained unfulfilled, and the Son of Man did not appear on the clouds of heaven, the Church had sufficient vitality to overcome the wide-spread disappointment. Faith in the risen Christ and the belief that each person now held within him- or herself the seeds of eternal life more than compensated for the as yet unrealised promise of a new world order. Besides, Christians, despite persecution, were able to adjust to the world as it actually existed. The Gospel stories, so it was believed, portrayed not fables and legends, but events that had taken place at a known place and time. The saving death and resurrection of Jesus, unlike such seemingly corresponding pagan myths as those of Orpheus, Osiris and Attis, could be attested by witnesses. Belief in them was so important as to be worth dying for. The kind of rational thought that had sapped the credibility of the Greek and Roman gods was now turned to the service of the Church. Men like Justin, Clement of Alexandria and Origen, by treating the unpalatable passages in the Old Testament as allegories, and universalising the person and message of Jesus, in Platonic and Stoic terms, made Christianity intellectually respectable.

Religion as a form of knowledge

Gnosticism—that is, Christian belief as a form of esoteric knowledge—came to be officially repudiated by the Church, in favour of a faith based on trust and the acceptance of ecclesiastical authority. But the deviations of the gnostics, with respect to the Incarnation, could not hide from the more thoughtful the fact that genuine religion has at its root a personal experience, an existential rebirth that cleanses the mind. The Pauline epistles (e.g., 2 Corinthians 4.6, Philippians 1.9) and the Fourth Gospel (e.g., John 8.28, 17.3) were there to show that the religion of Jesus demanded more than blind faith; it was in fact a form of *gnosis*, however liable to misunderstanding the word itself might be. The initiated, that is, baptised, Christian had a *knowledge* that outsiders apparently did not have. What that knowledge was, or more precisely, how it can be reinterpreted in terms of today, it is largely the purpose of the present essay to explore.

St John's gospel presents Jesus as the manifestation of ultimate truth, the truth which God is. The majority of persons interested in Jesus, however, have shown little concern to investigate questions of ultimate truth. The role of the Church, understandably enough, has been to articulate statements about him which can be considered 'true', and to devise forms of worship and a code of conduct appropriate to what is believed. To preserve intact, as an unchanging deposit, 'the faith which was once for all delivered to the saints', was the chief objective of the early ecclesiastical councils. Right belief, signified by a declared adherence to approved verbal formulas, eventually became the test of whether or not you were a Christian. Charity could flourish within the framework of orthodoxy; in its defence persecution and even death when necessary were patiently endured. If the love of the average Christian was hardly world-embracing, two reasons account for this. First, the Church had enlarged without abandoning the outlook taken over from Israel, that its members were a chosen people, the remainder of the human race not yet being of the elect. Secondly, the Church was struggling to discover her own identity, to mark herself off from Judaism on the one hand and from various pagan and heretical sects on the other. The time was not ripe to draw from the Judaeo-Christian belief in only one God the effective corollary that there could be only one world community.

The Christian establishment and philosophy

When in the fourth century Christianity became the established religion of the Roman Empire, the Church enjoyed the benefits of state support. Under Constantine and his successors it paid to be a Christian. In many cases conformity to the existing order rather than a sincere personal choice governed the situation. Even so, the call to spiritual rebirth, to something more soul-stirring than routine observance, was not to be denied. For many this took the form of flight from the corruption of the city to the solitude of the desert. Years before the conversion of Constantine the blessings of officialdom had brought, along with its favours, a sense that all was not well. It is doubtful whether the Roman ethical standards were higher under the first Christian emperors than they had been under the Antonines. Withdrawal from the allurements of society by the practice of asceticism became fashionable, and the arid spaces of Egypt were dotted with groups of monks dedicated to going it alone. The problems of how to combine world acceptance with spiritual detachment, responsibility to society with self-perfection, had still to be resolved.

Meanwhile among those given to reflective thought the question had arisen at least implicitly: Could the new religion offer a philosophy of life as satisfying to the human spirit as its current rivals, the varying forms of Stoicism and Platonism? Time would show that it could—if philosophy is regarded, not as a self-consistent intellectual system, the concern of academic specialists, but as the pursuit of wisdom and the path to the good and happy life. The chief contributions came from the Christian school at Alexandria, the

Cappadocian Fathers and, as affecting western Christendom, St Augustine of Hippo. He had been influenced by, among others, the Neoplatonists—the 'Platonici', as he called them. But the extent to which the abstractions of Platonic thought could bring out the deeper meaning of the Gospel was limited, and the domination of the western Church by its Augustinian inheritance has been a decidedly mixed blessing. Along with Augustine's penetrating genius went a strain of intolerance and disputatiousness, an intemperance of spirit that overstrained his logic; he never entirely rid himself of his earlier Manichaeism and he wrote so much on such a variety of topics that he could be appealed to as an authority by all the contending parties at the time of the Reformation and its aftermath.

Nevertheless a preoccupation with what he regarded as 'immutable truth' underlay Augustine's thinking. Nowadays, it should be remarked parenthetically, professional philosophers tend to limit discussions of truth to verbal statements in relation to demonstrable facts. Thus to say 'the grass is green' is to exemplify truth, and beyond variations of this kind of statement language borders on the meaningless. However, a long tradition of thought before and after Augustine, held that we can speak meaningfully of truth, not merely as applied to statements and self-evident facts, but as the *reality* of things (as what enables us to say, in the example cited, 'this is truly grass', not just the appearance of it, or something else altogether). This is metaphysical or onto-logical truth—a case of a concept of universal application, 'grassness' being exemplified. When the Fourth Gospel (14.6) records Jesus as saying 'I am . . . the truth', the reference is to timeless reality, the ground of being, which ultimately validates every 'true' statement and yet which cannot properly be represented in words at all. So at least Augustine understood the matter.

That the mind can know truth in any sense, he believed, is

due to a divine illumination; God is proved to exist by the fact that from no other source could truth arise in the mutable human intellect. Whether we say that seven plus three equals ten, or that wisdom is a knowledge that confers beatitude upon those who possess it, we do not simply know that it is so, we say that it cannot be otherwise. So St Augustine argues, to conclude that there are necessary, and therefore immutable, truths whose existence establishes the reality of God. Whatever may be thought of such a line of argument today, it points to an important fact of contemporary interest—the mind of Augustine and his theological successors was arrested by the question of truth in itself and for its own sake, not merely by truths of orthodoxy in so far as they served the interests of the Church.

When we consult the writings of that much misunderstood ninth-century theologian John the Scot (Johannes Scotus Erigena), we find him appealing to St Augustine in support of his view that: 'It is therefore certain that true religion is true philosophy, and, conversely, that true philosophy is true religion.' Faith focused upon scripture lies at the beginning of the Christian's religious inquiry; yet if error is to be avoided, scripture must be interpreted in harmony with reason. Faith is itself the principle from which the knowledge of the Creator begins to develop. Faith of its nature kindles in the mind an intellectual light which is none other than that of philosophy. This view of the matter has never been wholly acceptable to Church authority and it was later to be obliterated by Luther's anti-intellectualism; yet it is well to remember that, in an unenlightened age, John the Scot was an accomplished Greek scholar: he brought to the West a way of thought initiated by such theologians as the pseudonymous Denis the Areopagite and Maximus the Confessor. He offered the Latins a reasonable interpretation of biblical texts which had often been expounded with allegorical extravagance by St Ambrose and St Augustine. When God speaks, we have to believe, because what God says is true, whether we understand it or not. When a man speaks, even if his authority is universally recognised by other men, what he says is true only if reason approves it. Erigena's position here, as Etienne Gilson has pointed out, 'is a simple application of the principle, admitted by all mediaeval theologians, that God alone is infallible'.[1]

The Middle Ages

The movement initiated by Scotus Erigena barely survived its author. The tenth century had little to offer by way of spiritual enlightenment. Not until the appearance of Anselm of Canterbury (1033-1109) could western Christendom point to a thinker with a mind of sufficient scope to temper a strictly monastic ideal of the Christian life with the claims of secular culture. Vague memories of Greek humanism had survived sporadically in the cathedral schools of Britain and Gaul through the reign of Charlemagne. Had not Alcuin (730-804) cherished the ambition, in his own words, 'to build up in France a new Athens'—or to be more exact, an Athens that was Christian? So we find, rather more than two centuries later, a group of Benedictines who saw no opposition between religious faith and the free play of the mind. At Anselm's abbey of Bec certain monks desired a model for meditation on the existence and essence of God, in which everything would be proved by reason and where nothing would be based on scriptural authority. To this request Anselm replied with his *Monologium*. He refuses to submit holy scripture to philosophical dialectic: we must begin with faith as a starting point. One does not understand in order to believe, but on the contrary, one believes in order to understand. Given an initial belief, understanding not only may but should be pressed to the uttermost. Not to put faith

[1] Etienne Gilson, *History of Christian Philosophy in the Middle Ages* (Random House. New York, 1955), p. 115.

first is presumption; not to appeal to reason next is negligence.

Much that Anselm has to say is of more than historical interest. The contents of the Bible and the writings of the Church fathers, for all their value, cannot alter the fact that divine revelation is so vast and profound that mortals can never succeed in exhausting it. The Church is still in a state of comparative ignorance, always in need of being further enlightened. How far Anselm's insight and logical skill helped the process of enlightenment is nevertheless open to question. His instruments for elucidating scripture were practically confined to Aristotle's dialectic and the works of St Augustine. However learned a man of the eleventh century might be, he had little sense of history. No physics, no anthropology, no metaphysics (even Plotinus was unknown to Anselm), no system of rational ethics, were available to him.

Anselm's famous 'ontological argument' for God's existence amounts to no more than the claim that the concept of absolute being—that is to say, a being than which none more perfect can be thought—compels by the force of its own logic the affirmation of that being's existence. As Gilson has pointed out: 'This demonstration of the existence of God is assuredly the triumph of pure dialectic operating on a definition.'[1] Those who can accept that intelligible being conceived by thought must necessarily exist will find the argument persuasive; those who hold that any problem of existence can be solved only in the light of empirical evidence will remain unconvinced. Less unsatisfactory than either of these positions may be a viewpoint that transcends and so incorporates them both. The absolute cannot be conceived by thought or expressed in words, but given certain conditions, it can be *experienced*. What those conditions are we shall attempt to explain later. Meanwhile it seems safe to say that,

[1] *Op. cit.*, p. 133.

today as in the past, those who accept God as existing do so by an act of faith, rather than as convinced by rational argument.

No survey, however brief, of such elements of Christian thought as have their relevance today would be complete without mention of Peter Abelard (1079–1142). Best known to the world in general for his tragic love affair with Héloïse, he is widely acknowledged by students to have been the most brilliantly constructive mind in the Church between Scotus Erigena and Thomas Aquinas. Intellectually aggressive, with a taste for fishing in the troubled waters of contemporary dialectic, Abelard made many enemies and could hardly fail to fall foul of an authoritarian mystic of the type of St Bernard of Clairvaux. Yet Abelard's trust in the powers of reason and his logical method laid the foundations for the Catholic theological synthesis of the thirteenth century. William of Saint-Thierry and St Bernard might condemn his audacious probing of faith by reason as intellectual pride; they failed to appreciate that the surface combativeness concealed a clear mind and a generous heart. Christian revelation was never for Abelard an impassable barrier dividing the chosen from the condemened, truth from error.

Two points in particular indicate Abelard's capacity to clarify Christian thinking. First, his unshakable confidence in the catholicity of truth: even in that comparatively dark age he did not exclude either pagans or Jews from salvation; he anticipated the humane view of educated Christians in the sixteenth century—Erasmus, for example—that the lives of many of the Greek philosophers compared favourably with the Christian saints. Secondly, Abelard's explanation of the Redemption has an irresistible appeal. Compared to some of the legalistic theories of his predecessors, his focusing attention on the religion of Jesus, rather than religion about Jesus, touches the heart of the matter. We are redeemed if we exemplify in our own lives the pattern of living and dying set before us by Christ. The Cross and Resurrection are not simply saving events which happened 'out there'; they are salutary in so far as we accept Christ as our example. Liberation comes to the extent that we ourselves undergo a spiritual death and rebirth, suffer our own cross, enjoy our resurrection.

We come now for a moment to Thomas Aquinas. No one who has consulted the earlier work of the present writer will accuse him of underestimating the importance of St Thomas. Today, however, his contribution to Christian thought is in eclipse. To explain the reasons for this situation, or to try to change it, even if it were desirable to do so, would take us outside the scope of our inquiry. Two observations, however, may be in order. In the first place, theology in the thirteenth century had come to be regarded as a science teachable impersonally, in the same way as all the other arts and sciences. Its conclusions were thought to be 'objective'—that is to say, logical inferences drawn from propositions whose content was held to be revealed by God. Few of those interested in divinity would now claim that theology can still be satisfactorily handled in this way. Rather it should be seen to emerge from the personal experience of the theologian, as exemplified in the work of an Augustine, a Luther or Dietrich Bonhoeffer.

In the second place, it may be said that Thomas's theology, at its deepest level, is by no means as impersonal as is often alleged. No doubt it was his own experience that enabled him to achieve a concept of God much nearer to our modern understanding than it had been left by the Platonists and St Augustine himself. In Augustine's thought God was immutable and eternal 'being'; for Anselm the dominating notion was that of 'entity'. According to Thomas, in so far as the matter can be put into words at all, God's being is to be conceived not as a noun, an essence (*essentia*), but verbally as 'existence' (*esse*). God's being is to be understood in the fulness of its existential meaning—with the important proviso, however, that existence here is not a process, a projection from the present into the future. Being as here understood is outside all the categories, including those of space and time; it is the act which is the very core of all that is, inasmuch as it holds in existence whatever exists.

We can infer from our experience, according to Thomas, that the ultimate reality we call God accounts for all phenomena. But since we are unable to conceptualise a reality whose very essence is to exist, we cannot know God by direct intuition—at least in this life (which is all we shall be concerned with throughout these pages). Put another way, we may have a sense of the Divine manifesting itself in what we can see and hear and feel, but God cannot be an object of vision, whether physical or mental. Thus St Thomas in this respect, without being aware of it, is nearer to the Hindu theologian Shankara than he is to the Christian Anselm. For, as we shall see later, the advaita (i.e., non-dual) Vedanta teaches that union with God is not by way of mental concepts or even vision; it is an experience of *realisation* involving the whole personality.

Ecclesiastical thought-control and its limits

In 1277, three years after the death of St Thomas, the comparative freedom enjoyed by philosophers and theologians came to an end. The autocratic and impulsive Etienne Tempier, Bishop of Paris, proscribed 219 propositions, some of them touching Aquinas. The Dominican Robert Kilwardby, Archbishop of Canterbury, followed suit and Pope John XXI prescribed measures implementing the Paris condemnation. Not that these acts of Church authority initiated a new state of affairs: they were symptoms of an already existing reaction against what was felt to be the excessive intellectual independence of some masters in philosophy and theology. Inevitably the mental climate at such centres of learning as Paris and Oxford changed: dialectical caution replaced creative thinking—at least until philosophy repudiated altogether its mediaeval role as the handmaid of theology and reclaimed for itself complete autonomy. The golden age of scholasticism had passed.

We cannot leave the mediaeval scene, however, without reference to a personality whose influence today is very much alive, Meister Eckhart (1260–1327). His teaching is in part obscure and some of it was posthumously condemned by Pope John XXII as 'heretical and dangerous'; in consequence of which portions of his work are unavailable for study. None the less, anyone concerned to account for the contemporary interest in the 'experience of God', or to examine possible parallels between Christianity and the religions of India, cannot afford to neglect Eckhart.[1] His thought, though avowedly Christian, appears to be deeply imbued with Neoplatonism—itself quite possibly deriving from Persian, and even Indian, sources. He conceives God, not as do St Augustine and St Thomas, as *being*, but as something higher than being, namely, the 'One'.[2] Eckhart identifies the One with the act of understanding (*intellectus*) which, though the cause of being, cannot itself be called being. God, therefore, it would seem, is pure consciousness, unadulterated awareness. Here surely we have an echo of Aristotle's conception of the first unmoved mover as 'knowledge of knowledge'.

Creatures derive both their being and their power to understand (*intellectus*) from the One. The creature taken in itself is a nothing (*nulleitas*); it is no more than a manifestation of the divine fecundity. In proportion to its understanding,

[1] See the carefully documented parallels, and differences, between Shankara and Eckhart in Rudolph Otto, *Mysticism East and West*, originally published by the Macmillan Company, 1932, available in paperback, Meridian Books New York, 1957.

[2] The Neoplatonic 'one' is not to be regarded as the first of a numerical sequence; it is opposed to the 'many', cannot be categorised, and lies beyond the concept of 'being'.

its awareness, does it participate in the One, the Godhead. Eckhart, like Plotinus, holds that man returns to the One on which his being depends in virtue of knowledge, by an increasing awareness of his real situation. One of the propositions attributed to Eckhart and censured in 1329 was: 'There is in the soul something which is uncreated and uncreatable, and that is its intellect.'[1] In order to unite with God man has only to lock himself up in that 'citadel of the soul', where he is no longer distinguished from God, since there is a sharing in the One.

In all this Eckhart refused to concede to his critics—the most vociferous being members of a rival religious order—that he was unorthodox. He drew freely from the writings of Aristotle, Albert the Great and Thomas Aquinas, however subjectively he interpreted them. Eckhart's was a theology animated by a profound spiritual life; it mirrored, as it seemed to him, his personal experience. Since the soul in its inmost depths clings to the Deity, it can never be outside God, but it can either become attached to itself and so withdraw from him, or, on the contrary, it can become absorbed in that which is deepest within itself and thus become reunited in him. In understanding his ego to be nothing but a manifestation of the One, the God whom above all he loves, man at the same time finds his true self.

Perhaps the fairest comment at this point on the influence of Eckhart comes, once more, from Gilson: 'If an authentically Christian spiritual life had not been the nourishing soil of Eckhartian speculation, the doctrinal condemnations directed against it would have put an end to its history. But that is not what happened. The names and works of John Tauler (1300–1361), of Henry Suso (1300–1365) and of

---

[1] It should be noted that mediaeval theologians drew a clear distinction between intellect (*intellectus*) and reason (*ratio*). Intellect is the power of intuitive apprehension, reason the capacity to draw logical inferences from what is apprehended. Thus, broadly speaking, intellect is metaphysical, reason analytical.

John Ruysbroeck (1293–1381) testify to the lasting influence of Eckhart's doctrine on souls whose spiritual life was certainly very noble.'[1] When the time arrives—already envisaged by the Second Vatican Council—for what has been called 'the wider ecumenism', that is to say, a serious attempt at dialogue between Christianity and the religions of India, the basis for it cannot be the exoteric questions of doctrine and forms of worship which characterise most Christian interdenominational encounters. The point of contact will be what Leibniz was later to call the 'perennial philosophy', in which Catholic theology at its most enlightened has expressed itself. What is called for is a discriminating reappraisal of the tradition, touching human life at its deepest, which has come down from Denis the Areopagite, Scotus Erigena, Eckhart, to manifest itself in a fourteenth-century work like *The Cloud of Unknowing* and in the life of a saint so impeccably orthodox as St John of the Cross. Truth is more easily discovered by negating the false than by positive affirmations. We know more clearly what God is not than what he is. By approaching religious questions in this spirit we can learn for ourselves not only the inadequacy of ideas to conceive, or words to express, what we really mean, but also how carefully we must interpret the contents of the biblical revelation if we are not to be misled.

The first half of the fifteenth century witnessed in the work of one man the intimate union of philosophy and theology which brings to its logical conclusion the line of thought that has occupied us so far. It emerged in an unexpected quarter: from the mind of a bishop and cardinal of the holy Roman Church. Nicholas of Cusa (1401–1464) believed that if one is to think truly as a Christian he must achieve a fundamental unity among the various theological schools. This would come about, not by reconciling opposites, but by transcending the contradictions. Hence the need to break away from

[1] *Op. cit.*, p. 443.

the limitations of the Aristotelean dialectics in which even St Thomas was too much involved. What was needed was a return to the tradition of thought stemming from Plotinus. Unfortunately this manner of thinking—regarded as elementary by Hindu and Buddhist scholars—brings little satisfaction to minds less anxious to discover how fundamentally they are at one than to define the characteristics that make them different. For Nicholas, the Plotinian 'One' implied that God was 'infinite being', and this was the very object of Christian theology.

In his treatise *On Learned Unknowing* (*De docta ignorantia*) Nicholas teaches that the infinite as such is unknown, because between the truly infinite and anything finite there is no proportion; the infinite is the absolute and perfect blending of contraries (*coincidentia oppositorum*). Defending his position against its critics, he argues that learned non-knowledge was in fact the highest stage of intellectual apprehension accessible to the human mind, since the Truth, which is absolute, one and infinitely simple, is unknowable to man. Knowledge by contrast is relative, multiple, complex, and at best only approximate. The road to Truth therefore leads beyond the principle of contradiction and the processes of reason; it is only by intuition that we can discover God, the coincidence of opposites, wherein all contradictions meet. These assertions are intended to indicate that God may be regarded as at once infinitely great and infinitely small, the maximum and the minimum, the centre and the circumference of the universe, everywhere and nowhere, neither One nor Three, but Triune.

As a theologian, Nicholas was not in quest of a supreme concept virtually including all concepts; he wishes to reach beyond concepts, to overcome conceptual distinctions in the unity of an intuition. If we are to speak of God, the only way to eliminate concepts is by using negative terms, since according to Denis, and also in some degree Aquinas (who

qualified his Aristotleanism in divinity with the more con-
genial teaching of Denis the Areopagite), negative theology
provides the only kind of language applicable to the divine
transcendence. From this it does not follow that we cannot
be aware of God's presence, only that no concept or idea
formed by the human mind can yield any direct knowledge
of him.

It is hardly necessary to say that Nicholas of Cusa's
doctrine was viewed with suspicion in many quarters.
Acceptable as it may be to the philosophically minded that
statements of 'truth', however authoritative, have only a
relative value, those who prefer to have religion served to
them in dogmatic formulas could hardly be satisfied. Many
found more acceptable the nominalist views of John Gerson,
who had become chancellor of the University of Paris in
1395. He deplored what he considered the radical Platonism
of the natural theologies, which confound the Christian God
with the 'good' conceived as more or less analogous to nature.
The dominating aspect of God, according to Gerson, is free
will. Let us not therefore explore God's nature, which is
presumption; rather let us repent and seek to do his will.
'God does not will certain actions because they are good,'
Gerson affirms, 'but they are good because he wills them.'
How different is the God of the philosophers from the God
we find in scripture!

Towards the secularisation of Christianity

A debased scholasticism had brought the philosophical
approach to God into disrepute. Did not the *Imitation of
Christ*, a book which appeared during Gerson's lifetime, make
it clear that it was more profitable to have contrition than to
be able to define it? Philosophy was now largely restricted
to debates about definitions and logic. Theology considered
not so much God's truth and wisdom, as his will to save or
condemn. Both themes for reflection were sanctioned by the

Bible, both were represented in the works of St Augustine; but it was the latter that prevailed among the Augustinian hermits at Erfut, when in 1505 Martin Luther entered the monastery, in fulfilment of a vow made amid the terrors of a thunderstorm.

Of the monumental impact made by Luther on Christendom little can be said here. His insistence that human integrity comes as an unmerited gift on God's part, to be received in trusting faith, touches the heart of the matter. No amount of strenuous search can discover the pearl of great price. Being in such dire need, Luther deduced that humanity is by nature incapable of any virtue. Here he could find strong support in St Augustine. Against him lay the major part of Catholic tradition—shared in this respect, with even stronger emphasis, as we shall have occasion to note later, by Mahayana Buddhism. St Thomas had argued, more reasonably, that though clouded in mind and weakened in his will, man was in his nature essentially sound. God's grace did not cover over corruption; it brought a new impulse of life to what needed healing.

Luther's contribution can be considered in many respects constructive. Though his theology, more than that of most theologians, was a reflection of his own temperament and its difficulties, he had a liberating effect on his age. If the long-term result of his life-work was to make religion increasingly a matter of personal choice, that might eventually prove to be a benefit. He was a mediaeval man in revolt against the mediaeval Church. His deep emotions completely controlled his powers of judgement. He cherished doctrinal unity as earnestly as those who would have destroyed him. Which is perhaps only to say that he was confused in a series of highly confusing situations. Even today it is impossible to evaluate his work in terms of good or ill. The increasing dissensions among his adherents during his lifetime at least showed that for Christians the religious options were becoming wider.

The revolution begun by Luther put an end to what has been called Christendom's 'Constantinian era'; the Papacy, though clinging to its outward trappings, would never be the same again. The secularisation of Christianity was on its way. Luther rightly believed that the father of a family, the magistrate or the peasant, could be as much under God's favour as the monk in his monastery. The Protestant reformers were themselves mediaeval men, preoccupied with problems inherited from the middle ages, but implicit in their theology were ideas which, combining with other cultural developments, would slowly bring to birth the modern world. For good or ill, the Church was becoming a voluntary organisation for people interested in religion, instead of being the cultural bond which held society together. Historians have pointed out that the end of the mediaeval world came, not when Luther posted his ninety-five theses on the door of the castle church at Wittenberg, but with the peace of Westphalia (1648) which gave political effect well over a century later to the stalemate of the wars of religion. The institutional Church no longer had its unchallenged centre in Rome. The Lutheran, Calvinist and Anglican forms of the Reformation not only corresponded to geographical areas, they represented beliefs and life-styles sincerely upheld by those wholeheartedly pledged to Christianity. In view of the ferocity with which the wars of religion had been fought on the European continent, it occurred to many not blinded by bigotry that there might be a worse betrayal of the Christian gospel than any amount of heterodoxy. Church doctrine, once thought to be life-giving truth on which prayer and action could be securely based, began to be seen increasingly as a human structure, at odds with reality and needing to call upon authority precisely because it lacked intrinsic truth. The long-term result of the theological scepticism engendered by the religious wars was the widespread abandonment of any concept of the supernatural. By the early eighteenth century nature and the natural man were the ideas that dominated the minds of leading thinkers.

'This type of thought', writes William Nicholls in his admirable Pelican Original *Systematic and Philosophical Theology*,[1] 'disturbed the centuries old balance between nature and grace, philosophy and theology, reason and revelation, in favour of the first term of each of such pairs. Nature and the natural man were the great ideas that excited the men of the period. The natural was contrasted not just with the artificial in the sense of what is falsely sophisticated by civilization, but with the intellectual structures erected by theology in the name of revelation.' Subsequently there have been protests and reactions against this state of affairs, but in principle it still persists. It may be doubted whether the Church has even begun to come to terms with it.

From criticism to free religious choice

An honest admission of the facts by churchmen is indispensable if attempts at Christian renewal are to carry conviction. It is hard not to agree, in general terms, with the verdict of F. C. Happold who has written so much, wisely and well, in support of genuine Christianity:

> If one surveys the part secularism and humanism have played since the Renaissance, one cannot but feel that it has been a beneficent one. It has been, not the Christian Church, but the scientists and humanists who have led the advance in the march towards toleration and free enquiry and towards social justice and a better life for the common man. In spite of its saints, mystics, and martyrs, the history of the Christian Church is a sorry one. It is far too much the story of intolerance, persecution and bigotry, of inquisitions, torture and burnings, of 'images' of God which had little resemblance to the loving Father or our Lord Jesus Christ, or to the inner

[1] Penguin Books, 1969, p. 36.

Christ of St Paul. One can sympathize with the couplet in
Martin Skinner's satirical poem:
And God in welcome smiled from Buddha's face,
Though Calvin in Geneva preached of grace.[1]

Two further continuing events were to frustrate the efforts
of those who still strove to present the case for Christianity in
the form of dogmatic pronouncements. The first was the
development of a critical approach to history, particularly as
this applied to the contents of the Bible. The second was the
all-pervasive effects of scientific technology and the theories
of the structure of the universe on which that technology was
based. Close study of the biblical material revealed that there
was comparatively little to be found in the Old Testament
that could be regarded as historically reliable, or even
ethically edifying. Today Jewish and Christian scholars
claim that these writings retain their importance, not as
accurate records of what actually happened, but on account
of their theological meaning. Whether that meaning emerges
in every case from an impartial study of the text, or has been
imposed upon it in virtue of scholarly or religious preconceptions, is a question that is still under review.

As for the New Testament, it soon became apparent that
the gospels were based on earlier written sources and that
their authors were not eyewitnesses of the events they record.
Our present texts could not have been composed earlier than
a generation, perhaps two generations, after the lifetime of
Jesus. The Pauline epistles, besides being earlier than the
gospels, were not originally written for general publication;
their purpose was to convey to various local churches St
Paul's understanding of the significance of the crucifixion
and resurrection of Jesus, in whose Galilean and Judean
ministry Paul had curiously little interest. In the light of
these and other related findings, the conclusion was hard to

[1] F. C. Happold, *Religious Faith and Twentieth-Century Man*, Penguin Books,
1966, p. 29.

escape that the Jesus of history, as distinct from the Christ of faith, may have been very different from the picture of him presented by popular piety.

If Christianity is to survive the challenge of a scientific age, it can hardly do so by basing its claims on memories of the past or expectations for the future. Variations on the theme of the quest for the historical Jesus, or exercises in a recently devised 'theology of hope', may illustrate how far Catholic thought has sunk from the days when its exponents could have talked on equal terms with a Plato or Aristotle. Understandably the official Church cannot initiate the task of re-thinking her message from its foundations, lest she appear to be modifying the belief system adhered to by the unreflecting Christian majority. What Church authority can do, however —and, happily, appears to be doing—is to recognise the problems and how urgent is the need for their informed discussion.

Christian sociologists tell us that today's is not a secularist but rather a post-secularist world. The average man and woman is not less religious than in past ages; he or she is religious with a difference. The questions now are not: What has been revealed? What is the content of 'the faith once delivered to the saints'? But—does it matter? And assuming that it does, what does it mean? Considered within its conceptual framework, every religion may be regarded as the basic symbol system of its respective adherents. Conversely, a person's basic symbol system is for all practical purposes his or her religion. Thus a multiplicity of religious choices present themselves. Besides a fragmented Christianity (for which 'ecumenism' is another name), Judaism in its various forms, Hinduism, Buddhism, Sufism and other accepted claimants, we have agnosticism, secular humanism, nature worship, Marxism and psycho-analysis, to name but a few of the refuges in which people seek a solution to life's problems—or salvation, to use the old-fashioned language of religion.

Such a conclusion need not prove as daunting to a Christian's will to believe as it might appear. What is implied may turn out to be no more than a call to look a little deeper, to open the mind to a wider perspective. Over thirty years ago the Hindu scholar Sarvepalli Radhakrishnan observed: 'The indifference to organised religions is the product not so much of growing secularism as of deepening spirituality. Scrupulous sensitiveness in our search for truth is making it difficult for us to accept doubtful authority or half-heard traditions. If genuine religious belief has become for many a phenomenon of the past, it is because religions confound eternal truth with temporal facts, metaphysics with history. They have become largely a traffic with the past.'[1] These words, besides suggesting a clue to much that is to follow here, seem as pertinent today as when they were first written.

[1] S. Radhakrishnan, *Eastern Religions and Western Thought*, Oxford University Press, 1940, pp. 58–59.

2 The church: a haven for conformists?

WHAT PART can a 'scrupulous sensitiveness in the search for truth' play in the life of a faithful member of the Christian Church? Does not his very acceptance of the faith imply that, with regard to the answer to life's deepest questions, for him the search is at an end? Theoretically this may be so, and even in practice a Christian may choose to close his mind to further speculation and strive to live by the light that has so far been given him. But for many, perhaps the majority, the urge to further truth-seeking cannot be denied. What do I *mean* when I say that I believe? The ancient name for the Christian creeds was 'symbol'—a Greek word meaning a 'sign': in this case a verbal sign for some unseen reality. Inevitably, therefore, even when we accept the sign, the question of what precisely it refers to remains. Belief must seek understanding—and religious understanding, whatever some linguistic philosophers may say, lies beyond sense perception, in metaphysical intuition.

The claim that Christianity is a religion bound up with history—a claim that is commonly regarded as a strong point in its favour—is only a half truth. Jesus the man was an historical figure, Jesus the Logos of God is outside time and beyond history. 'Before Abraham was I am' (John 8.58). It is of some importance that the crucifixion and resurrection actually happened as matters of record, but the eternal

meaning of these events is of infinitely greater importance.
The modern preoccupation with historical research, as
applied to the New Testament, is only slightly more helpful
in disclosing its message than a fundamentalist biblical
literalism. The early Church Fathers, who were more at
home in the world in which the gospels and the Pauline
epistles were written than we are today, recognised four ways
of interpreting the scriptures: the literal or historical, the
moral, the allegorical and the spiritual—and they were over-
whelmingly interested in the last three. The ablest Catholic
theologians, notably St Thomas, held that the central
Christian truths were not the object of historical research;
they were the focus of a faith intent on a revelation coming
from God as *veritas prima*, the first truth. On this view—
largely lost sight of today even by Catholics—the response
appropriate to the believer is contemplation in the present
rather than recollections of the past.

It would be an oversimplification to pretend that this can
be the whole story. How the New Testament writings were
understood by those who first heard and read them, though
not now of paramount importance, still remains of great
interest. The contrast with the Hindu-Buddhist tradition at
this point is worth noting. In the words of an eminent
orientalist, Ananda K. Coomaraswamy, 'The Mahayanist
believer is warned—precisely as the worshipper of Krishna is
warned in the Vaishnavite scriptures that the Krishna Lila
is not a history, but a process for ever unfolded in the heart
of man—that matters of historical fact are without religious
significance'.[1] Here we are taken too far in the non-historical
direction. What actually happened in the world of space and
time can be of immense significance, if it is a means whereby
men are delivered from selfishness and attain a state of being
beyond the temporal order. Yet it seems fair to say that for

---

[1] Quoted from Aldous Huxley, *The Perennial Philosophy*, Harper & Brothers,
New York and London, 1944, 1945, p. 51.

St Paul, the death and resurrection of Christ, besides being historic facts, are also intended to be 'a process for ever unfolded in the heart of man'.

The Christian Church as it now exists is a complex of metaphysical and symbolic elements on the one hand, and historical and legal elements on the other. The first pair express the Church's vertical, timeless, universal dimensions; the second those that are linear or horizontal, temporal and local. These two sets of characteristics, representing respectively the treasure and the earthen vessels in which it is embodied (cf. 2 Corinthians 4.7), are inseparable from the Church as she exists in space and time. The first set concerns the life of the spirit, the second its outward manifestation. The first is the area of freedom, the second that of authority: under which arise the emotions of fear and hope—fear lest one transgress, hope for the realization of the 'glorious liberty of the children of God' (Romans 8.21). The emotions of fear and hope (in the sense of looking forward expectantly to a brighter future) are linked to the human condition, but they tend to diminish and even disappear as the truth of God's presence is realised and we are aware that the future, which can only become actual as the present, falls likewise under the divine providence. The authoritative aspect of the Church is chiefly that under which she presents herself as an historical phenomenon—appealing in that guise to some, unattractive to others. The philosophical theologians whose work we touched on in the last chapter were on the whole interested in the Church's metaphysics and symbolism; within these spheres they were unquestionably truth-seekers. For those less gifted, or without the time for personal investigation—in a word, the ordinary faithful—truth as provided by the verbal formulations of the institutional Church sufficed.

What the institution embodied is 'without spot or wrinkle' (Ephesians 5.27), but the institution itself has the limitations of every corporate structure; it is subject to change and decay. We have already noted that Christendom as a cultural matrix of ideas and values and ethical convictions, to be applied over the widest area of human life, disappeared with the middle ages. But the Church as a society, in which all its members supposedly share a Christian faith, still precariously exists. The Lutheran, Calvinist and Anglican forms of the Reformation, along with Rome itself, as the latter has been obliged reluctantly to admit, together make up western Christianity. The treatment by the official Church of heretics and dissenters is too painfully well known to need recalling. Nevertheless that the Christian message, as so far understood, does not represent total truth has almost always been acknowledged in practice. From the fifth century onwards the Catholic Church could have condemned all philosophical speculation, including the actual study of philosophy, as being opposed to orthodox belief. Priests and monks could have been forbidden by ecclesiastical authority to open schools and teach doctrines that had been taught by pagans at a time when the Gospel had not yet been preached to the gentiles. The Popes could have condemned all efforts to achieve any understanding of faith by means of philosophical inquiry. Only no such thing happened during the middle ages: so that by the thirteenth century, as we have seen, Christianity could appear, within its prescribed limits, both as a vehicle of future salvation and a life-style adjusted to the realities of the known world.

Christian witness today: conversion and conformity

For reasons we have briefly outlined, all that has changed. It is doubtful whether the average Catholic could now give any clear answer to the question: what does 'salvation' mean? A posthumous state of future bliss 'in heaven'—is not a response likely to satisfy the critically minded, let alone the unthinking majority, of Christians. Their interest, like that of everybody else, is in how they are to live profitably, and if possible happily, in the present. Churchmen's well-intentioned efforts to be helpful do not appear, generally speaking, to inspire much confidence. Their preoccupation with sexual mores, usually in terms of negation, and their incapacity to stem the tide of economic exploitation, violence, bloodshed and war, account for the alienation of millions of young people from the institutional Church. More to the point perhaps, effective Christian witness has passed from the official ecclesiastical centres to the circumference: to groups of dedicated laymen and women, to religious communities deeply concerned for the life of the spirit, with prayer and meditation, to individuals who know when to be silent and when to speak, who can remove the scales from people's eyes in the light of their own knowledge, who are treading the path of wisdom and active compassion, and who accordingly can offer genuine enlightenment instead of a mere exposition of received religious opinions.

Yet the Church still powerfully appeals. At one level of human need she attracts in virtue of her exclusiveness: here alone is spiritual security, here alone the effective means of grace, here presumably and not elsewhere are the 'people of God'; here even, Rome claims (though now, wisely, in subdued tones) is infallible truth. Conversions to the Catholic Church are neither as numerous nor as fashionable as they were one or two generations ago, when the Church's more explicit authoritarianism and institutional strength exercised an almost political fascination over many minds whose sympathies were conservative and to the right of centre. Perhaps this is just as well. Conversions in the past have sometimes conveyed a misleading impression of both the converted and the Church that they joined. Ambiguity surrounds the description of a conversion to Catholicism in such terms as ' "entry into the world of guilt and sorrow:" the Catholic world of Graham Greene'. A harsher verdict emerges from Julian Jebb's basically approving account, in the *New Statesman*, of the work of Evelyn Waugh:

> After a broken first marriage he chose to find his truth in the Catholic Church. A suffocating aura of exclusiveness, sentimentality and guilt-expiation adhered to the practice of Roman Catholicism by members of the English upper classes from around 1930, the year of his conversion, right up to the end of the 1950s. They 'ganged-up' and mutually encouraged each other in the same way that Evelyn Waugh himself found so distasteful among the left-wing writers of the time . . . *Brideshead Revisited*, Waugh's poorest large-scale book, remains a cautionary memorial to his faith. By the time he came to write his masterpiece, *Sword of Honour*, his religious beliefs had fallen into place in a way which allowed him to incorporate them artistically into his work.

Humorously a similar point is made in a novel by Aldous Huxley:

> Meanwhile, look what had happened to poor Tom! Second Secretary at Tokyo; First Secretary at Oslo; Counsellor at La Paz; and now back, more or less for good, in the Foreign Office, climbing slowly up the hierarchy, towards posts of greater responsibility and tasks of increasing turpitude. And as the salary rose and the morality of what he was called upon to do correspondingly sank, the poor fellow's uneasiness had increased, until at last, with the row over Abyssinia, he just hadn't been able to stand it any longer. On the brink of resignation or a nervous breakdown, he had managed, in the nick of time, to get himself converted to Catholicism. Thenceforward, he had been able to pack up the moral responsibility for his share in the general iniquity, take it to Farm Street and leave it there, in camphor, so to speak, with the Jesuit Fathers. Admirable arrangement! It had made a new man of him. After fourteen years of childlessness, his wife had suddenly had a baby—conceived, Jeremy had calculated, on the very night the Spanish Civil War began. Then, two days after the sack of Nanking, Tom had published a volume of comic verse. (Curious how many English Catholics take to comic versifying.) Meanwhile, he was steadily gaining weight; between the *Anschluss* and Munich

he had put on eleven pounds. Another year or two of Farm Street and power politics, and Tom would turn the scale at fourteen stone and have written the libretto of a musical comedy.[1]

Biased and unfair as these observations may be, they are worth quoting for the grain of truth that usually underlies most caricatures. The 'great Church' of the west is still worth converting to, for the sacred tradition she represents, her relatively enlightened forms of religious practice, and the perennial philosophy (in its original meaning of 'love of wisdom') which, though temporarily eclipsed in a cloud of ecclesiological and scriptural discussion, she preserves. But the aftermath of Vatican II must by now have dispelled any illusions that psychological problems can be finally solved, or the quest for truth ended, by joining the Roman Church. Catholicism, I believe, still offers the western world the securest platform from which to launch a personal quest for ultimate religious meaning. It is also a safe resting place for those who feel no such urge.

No less an authority than John Henry Newman lends his sanction to just such a position. As William James has pointed out: 'Newman's imagination so innately craved an ecclesiastical system that he can write: "From the age of fifteen, dogma has been the fundamental principle of my religion: I know no other religion: I cannot enter into the idea of any other sort of religion." And again, speaking of himself about the age of thirty, he writes: "I loved to act as feeling myself in my Bishop's sight, as if it were the sight of God." '[2] Not every member of the clergy, even among the most dedicated, would echo these sentiments today. Until those chiefly responsible can present their message to the faithful as a one to one equation of salvation with reality and

---

[1] Aldous Huxley, *After Many a Summer Dies the Swan* (New York: Avon Paperbacks, 1952), pp. 159–160.
[2] *Apologia*, 1897, pp. 48, 50. Quoted from William James, *The Varieties of Religious Experience*, Fontana Library, Collins, 1960, pp. 439–440.

truth, the decline of the Church's influence is likely to continue.

Teaching authority carries little weight unless the teachers are still willing to be learners. This axiom is as applicable to the highest ecclesiastics as it is in the school room. In fact it is more applicable, since the school teacher has normally at least a limited mastery of his or her subject, whereas the churchman from the nature of the case can advance no such claim; and, if he is also an administrator, is probably out of touch with the available areas of knowledge open to the scholar and theologian. Yet the need for the faithful to be educated in the realities of religion was never more urgent. The concept of the mature Christian can usefully be substituted for that of the 'good Catholic'; the faith of adults can no longer survive on notions inculcated in childhood. Implicit in the Church's creeds is the premise that all language about God is inadequate; the creeds are like a finger pointing to the moon, not to be confused with the moon itself. Every attempt to lay down general moral principles needs to be modified by the proviso that circumstances alter cases. Would these reminders beget a sense of spiritual insecurity? The answer here, I think, is that only a false security can be generated by reliance on external authority. Attractive as is the prospect of knowing just where one is in religious matters, it is precisely this knowledge that no human teacher can supply. 'I know whom I have believed' (2 Timothy 1.12) refers to a state of mind enlightened by the Spirit, not to a conviction that what someone has said about God must be true.

The available evidence for the validity of the Church's claims now lies to hand for anyone who chooses to investigate the matter. Thus there is hardly anything that Church officials can tell the educated Christian layman that he cannot tell himself; and it is better that way. He is likely to learn from his priests and ministers more by what they are than from anything they have to say. There are grounds for believing that preachers attach considerably more importance to their sermons than do the congregations who are obliged to hear them. The clergy, like every professional body, has its own specialised interests: such as Church authority's latest 'terminological rulings', or the drawing up of inter-denominational 'agreed statements', yet these discussions are of little concern to the majority of Christians. They would be happy to hear less about the Church and more of God, and in particular, how they are to achieve the unifying knowledge of God manifested in Christ, which is itself the heart of Christianity.

Of greater consequence than the Church's internal debates is the Christian's attitude to the two revolutions—one of thought, the other of action—which are going on in the world at the present time. Together they could combine to clarify, at least by negation, the goal of the religious quest. The first revolution results from the long-term impact of the work of Marx and Freud. For Marx, whose effects may be the more enduring, religion was the product of a defective understanding that prevented people from coming to grips with the evils of their society. For Freud, religion was an illusion or projection that impaired self-knowledge and rendered people incapable of dealing with their own problems. It would be idle to pretend that a measure of truth does not underlie these judgements. The second revolution, that of action, which is largely Marxian inspired, may yet bring about the nuclear holocaust. It is the egalitarian movement towards the classless society, from three worlds to only one: which is a part of Christianity's message, however strongly it may be resisted by Christians both corporately and individually.

As is to be expected, these prospects are much more readily faced by the younger generation than by their elders. A characteristic of many young Catholics in their attitude towards the institutional Church is not scepticism or hostility, merely boredom and apathy. What she has to offer is *déjà vu*; they have heard it all before. There are few signs of anti-clericalism; what is called for is a different kind of clergy. Not authority figures with a sense of status, but simple Christians who are open and available and ready to serve. The time may be approaching when priests in their minis-terial capacity will become rather like doctors and lawyers—not taking the initiative but ready to answer calls for their professional services: to celebrate the Eucharist or administer the sacraments. Their leadership will be in response to demands and opportunities; its success will depend on such obvious factors as knowledge, energy, tact, and above all on their capacity to be wisely compassionate. Always, especially with the young, they will be teachers, but again, more by what they are than what they say. How agreeably the Church would be transformed, and how much closer to the spirit of the Gospel, if her leaders would take to heart the 2,500 year-old wisdom of the Chinese sage, the legendary Lao Tzu: 'As for the best leaders, the people do not notice their existence. The next best, the people honour and praise. The next, the people fear; and the next, the people hate. If you have no faith people will have no faith in you, and you must resort to oaths. When the best leader's work is done the people say: "We did it ourselves".'

Our eyes should be on the young: for they are the teach-able ones, as they are often unconscious teachers themselves. Many of them already have an understanding that this is one world. Often the young people of Europe and America are nearer to the youth of Africa and Asia than to their own parents and teachers. They are in no need of being told that if there is only one God there can be only one human com-munity. Not that they have any desire to see what are obvious cultural differences swamped by an international 'great Church'. Community living must first be practised on a small scale, so arranged as to allow each of its members at times to be alone, fulfilling a person's twofold need: to belong and to be on one's own. The interest now is in loosely structured communities, as open and free as possible, their few necessary rules being reached on a basis of mutual agreement, with honesty and truth and loving-kindness as their ideals. In this context, but perhaps only here, wisdom requires that we should all be conformists; for then we shall be conforming to 'that perfect law, which is the law of freedom' (James 1.25).

3

The challenge from the East

THE IMPORTANCE of the religions originating in India is becoming increasingly widely recognised in the West—though probably more so in America and on the European continent than in England, where our native insularity leaves us in the grip of theological inertia. The still weighty influence of the Anglican establishment combined with an unenterprising Roman Catholicism may largely account for this state of affairs. Serious students as well as hippies take themselves off to India, Nepal and points further east while the Christian clergy look on, defensive or vaguely anxious. The Churches are now so insecure that they have an understandable reluctance to expose themselves to what might prove a radical challenge to accepted modes of thought. Courses on comparative religion available in the universities, instead of being handled by representative insiders, are not seldom offered by the religiously indifferent or by conventional Christians, for whom the study of Hinduism and Buddhism is clearly a subordinate interest. When books on these subjects attract attention, it is usually ill-informed or nervously hostile. Even the *Times Literary Supplement*, to say nothing of the Catholic journals, apparently cannot find reviewers able to evaluate such work unpolemically, with sympathy and sufficient knowledge.

Yet many convinced Christians are now learning the

techniques of yoga or practising meditation in a form derived from Zen Buddhism. They have discovered, with Rudolph Otto, what is no longer open to dispute, that 'a lofty and advanced theism and not a "heathenish polytheism" is the basis upon which the mystic speculation of India rises'. Numbers of the younger generation, while dedicating their lives wholeheartedly to Christ in monasteries and convents and less structured religious communities, are finding that the traditional round of public worship and private prayer are somehow not enough to generate the degree of alert responsiveness demanded by their own religion in today's world. Can these innovations, and more important, the philosophy which underlies them, be assimilated by Christianity without changing its very nature? Here the answer may prove of greater consequence than reaching finality in many of the current discussions within the Church. For these are generally focused on ways and means of making human society more genuinely Christian; whereas those who turn to eastern religions are often seeking to resolve a more basic problem: whether Christianity itself, at least as it is commonly proclaimed, provides adequate answers to the fundamental religious questions. Widespread clerical ignorance of what attracts so many young people to the religions of the East could have serious results: chief among them being either the abandonment of religion altogether, or the delusion that Christians can only find elsewhere what is actually latent within their own tradition.

Western and Eastern religion

We may recall briefly the chief differences between the Judaeo-Christian tradition of the western world and the Hindu-Buddhist tradition of India and the Far East. The break between Christianity and Judaism had its parallel in the break between Buddhism and Hinduism, or rather of the Buddha with the teaching and practice of the Brahmin priesthood. Each turned on a living personality: in the first case, Jesus the Messiah; in the second case, Gautama the Buddha. Each religion, too, was eventually to flourish outside the land of its birth. Yet there is probably a greater continuity between Buddhism and the Hinduism from which it spring than there is between Christianity and Judaism.

> The more superficially one studies Buddhism, the more it seems to differ from the Brahmanism in which it originated; the more profound our study, the more difficult it becomes to distinguish Buddhism from Brahmanism, or to say in what respects, if any, Buddhism is really unorthodox. The outstanding distinction lies in the fact that Buddhist doctrine is propounded by an apparently historical founder, understood to have lived and taught in the sixth century BC. Beyond that there are only broad distinctions of emphasis.[1]

Buddhism, like Christianity, has its various divisions and sects. The Theravada (or Hinayana) might be compared roughly to Protestantism, the Mahayana to Catholicism. What marks the continuity in the Judaeo-Christian tradition, and distinguishes it from that of the Hindu Vedanta and the Buddhist Mahayana, is first, the emphasis on history as a factual sequence of events, and secondly the belief in the transcendent otherness of God.[2] Such contemporary Christian concepts as 'salvation history' and 'eschatology', which are believed to have a temporal as distinct from a mythical and timeless content, are not easily paralleled in Indian religion. Christianity teaches that the gulf between God as creator and humanity as created is so great that it can only be bridged by the incarnation of God himself in the person of Jesus of Nazareth—whose life, death and resurrection are the means to the world's salvation. Whether the differences

---

[1] Ananda K. Coomaraswamy, *Hinduism and Buddhism*, Philosophical Library, New York, p. 45.

[2] For an elaboration of these points the reader may be interested in my *The End of Religion—Autobiographical Explorations*, Harcourt Brace Jovanovich, New York and London, 1971, particularly Chapter 6, 'Promptings from India', pp. 103–200.

between these two, the greatest existing religious traditions, are as marked as they appear to be is a question we have yet to examine. Before doing so, however, let us consider some aspects of Christianity which may prepare our minds for a sympathetic encounter with Buddhist thought.

Routine Christianity

It is not usual, or very acceptable to churchmen, to distinguish between the exoteric and what is esoteric in the Christian tradition. The esoteric is often associated with some hidden understanding of Jesus' life-work into which he supposedly initiated his earliest followers. Leaving aside this possibility, for which there is little substantial evidence, we shall use 'esoteric' in our present context merely to indicate the implicit, what is most inward, in the Church's proclamation. The distinction is a useful one, since the Christian message as preached from the pulpit is not only ignored by the world at large, but for the faithful few listening in the pews it falls upon ears deadened by over-familiarity. Such is emphatically the case with many, perhaps the majority, of teenagers. Where religion holds their interest, it is not in terms of what it has to tell about the past or promise for the future; their concern is with what, if anything, the Church has to offer by way of enlightenment to the individual in his or her present situation. Or to be more precise: in what way religion today both fulfils one's potentialities as a person and confers that sense of belonging, of being one with a community, without which no amount of individualistic piety is of much value. Thoughts about the historic past activate the memory, a vision of the future (in so far as it is believed) may arouse hope: neither of which in themselves bring us nearer to the heart of religion—which is an experience of the living God. That can only happen in the present moment, in what St Augustine called the 'eternal now'.

We do not have to turn to eastern religions to discover

statements of this truth. They can be found in the New Testament and in the writings of many Christian saints. Where religion as an actual experience is not so easily discoverable is in the Church's routine teaching or in the daily conduct of the faithful. For practical purposes Catholicism is often reduced to the obligation to accept the traditional creeds, to attend Mass and receive the sacraments, to observe the moral virtues, to be loyal to ecclesiastical authority. The need to love God and one's neighbour is of course continually stressed, as also the necessity for personal prayer. If this programme and its full implications were understood in depth there might still be dissatisfaction, but the Church would be in a healthier state. Yet some underlying difficulties remain. Let us scan the items just mentioned briefly one by one.

Without questioning the validity of the creeds, we may recall the always pertinent fact that, however sacrosanct, they inadequately represent the realities they refer to. Creedal statements are not revelation, but mental concepts embodied in words about what is revealed. Thus it is possible to give assent to the creeds without one's personal relationship to God being affected. Accordingly there is point to Archbishop William Temple's paradoxical remark: 'I don't believe in the creeds, I believe in God'; itself an echo of St. Thomas's well known position: 'the act of belief does not terminate at the articles of the creed, but at that to which the articles relate.' The Church's liturgy and sacraments presuppose for their appreciation, first that their significance has been well understood, and secondly that those taking part are by temperament responsive to symbolic forms of worship, which is not by any means always the case. Today these conditions are hard to fulfil. The state of the Catholic liturgy is now confused, since the ancient tradition of worship has been rendered unstable by various attempts to make it appealing to contemporary taste. Moreover in a scientific age people look for possibilities of experimental contact with the realities of religion rather than have them mediated through symbols. As for morality: the virtuous life is hardly a peculiar monopoly of the Church; it is a condition of any form of wholesome living, while at the same time it points to what is beyond itself. Love of God and love of one's neighbour are indeed the heart of the matter, nourished as it must be by prayer, understood as a continuous living in the Divine presence. But here we reach the regions of the spirit, an area of freedom for which no human authority can legislate.

Christianity, as it is concerned with God and Jesus Christ, can hold its own; these preoccupations are of as much interest, at least among the thoughtful, as they have ever been. It is the Church as an agent of the Christian message that is in trouble. Why? Perhaps the basic reason is a deeply theological one: the Church's true raison d'être is to manifest to the world the Spirit of God, by which the Church claims to be animated. But the Spirit is like the wind, blowing where it pleases (John 3.8); it is too fluid to be bound within juridical structures, too elusive to be tied to any form of words. So the Church's representatives, carrying the treasure in earthen vessels, can only do their best. The Second Vatican Council, as an ecclesiastical exercise, exemplified what that best can be. Besides stimulating religious thought in terms of contemporary realities, the Council pointed the way to how the Church might come to a deeper understanding of herself and promote greater freedom among her members. So far as Christianity can be conveyed in words, the Council could hardly have done more. But therein lies the problem: the Church must speak—'the word of God', for that is the Church's mission. Yet the Word which *is* God, which became flesh (John 1.14), cannot be spoken by man. And the personal discovery, as a living experience, of this Word can alone give reality to religion.

Perhaps one of the lessons we are learning from the
Council is to be rather more modest about what the Church
has to offer by way of insight into the human condition. At
the level of authoritative pronouncements, or even at that of
the average Sunday sermon, churchmen have apparently
little that is new to say. Not the deficiencies of Christianity,
but the inherent limitations of the ministry of the word and
the sacraments, are what are now becoming evident. Both
words and sacraments are basically symbols: so that we need
to remind ourselves that to fail to distinguish between the
symbol and what is symbolised is to encourage a form of
idolatry. Many young people, though they may not define
it in these terms, are fully aware of this situation. They feel
that what is going on in church, for all the pious rhetoric that
is expended in commending it, is shallow and therefore
boring, since it provides no sense of immediacy. They fail to
see its relevance to their lives as they are actually lived.
Instead, they gather together in groups, to pray and to open
their minds and hearts to what they trust are the direct
promptings of the Holy Spirit, or perhaps to celebrate the
Eucharist in a friendly, intimate setting, such as characterised
the gathering at the Lord's original supper. Alternatively,
dissatisfied, they abandon the Church altogether: those in
search of excitement often take to drugs or some form of
occultism; those who seek a more lasting transformation of
consciousness may find it, even in a manner compatible with
their Christian upbringing, in Buddhist meditation.

Nonetheless, from the standpoint of traditional Christianity, the Church still has an arresting message to deliver: a
message which will be delivered the more effectively to the
degree that she abandons corporate egotism and ceases to
talk about herself. The primary need, I believe, is not an
adaptation of the Church's teaching to the supposed requirements of the modern mind, but a prolonged theological
meditation on the nature of Christian spirituality. Such an

investigation would clearly bring us back to the New Testament, with special reference to the Pauline epistles and the Fourth Gospel. From there we should pass to early Christian writers like St Justin and Clement of Alexandria, who were at pains to make clear that all truth, whatever its immediate source, comes from the Holy Spirit. The doctrines attributed to Origen, of metempsychosis and the final salvation of the whole human race, along with certain opinions of John Scotus Erigena and Meister Eckhart which later incurred official disfavour, are at least as worthy of serious reappraisal as the Catholic condemnation of Luther in the sixteenth century. The tradition of fundamental religious thinking exemplified by these writers was represented, in part at least, by Athanasius, Augustine, the pseudononymous Denis the Areopagite, Thomas Aquinas, the author of *The Cloud of Unknowing* and John of Ruysbroeck, without attracting unfavourable attention from the ecclesiastical authorities.

In this context I have designedly employed the phrase 'theological meditation', in order to distinguish what is called for from mere scholarly study. The term 'mystical' is perhaps unavoidable, being sanctioned by long usage, though 'metaphysical', as pertaining to the effort to come to grips with what lies beyond that which is perceptible by the senses, seems preferable. Impatient westerners who regard speculation turning on mysticism and metaphysics as so much moonshine should re-examine, if not their own thought processes, at least the evidence before them. Unfortunately those who have difficulty at this point include many sincere Christians, not excepting scholars and theologians. The reason for this, as Paul Tillich among others has pointed out, is because the intellectual climate of our day is permeated by nominalism. Minds so conditioned need to be liberated from particularities before they can make sense of the Platonic idealism, or its sequel, Mediaeval realism, in terms of which classical Christian theology was formulated. Here it may be enough to suggest that behind the question of fact, or even of truth, lies the question of meaning; and meaning for each individual person depends on the subjective interpretation of his or her experience, which can only be a metaphysical process. It is noteworthy that the writers mentioned above, from Athanasius to Ruysbroeck, though plentiful in their references to scripture, were but little concerned with Christianity in its historical setting. Jesus the Son of God presented the divine-human encounter in its fullest implications. How could this be explained? What did it amount to, not as a spectacle to be observed or an event to be thought about, but as a *reality* in the experience of every Christian? The possibilities latent in this area are of perennial importance: that they have been largely lost sight of perhaps accounts for the lifelessness of much contemporary religion.

The Incarnation

As might have been expected, it is at its central point that Christianity makes contact with the religions of the East. Too often Christians rest content, for all practical purposes, with the view that the Incarnation is a once-for-all event that took place at a certain point in history. He who became incarnate has now ascended to heaven and is to be worshipped as Lord. True—but how meagrely this reflects the full Christian revelation! Where are the echoes of the Pauline doctrine that life itself is Christ (Galatians 2.20, Philippians 1.21)? Or of the Johannine teaching that Christians are intended to be one with the Father in the way that Christ is (John 17.21–22)? As God became man, so man is to become God—such is the teaching of St Athanasius, the great defender of orthodoxy at the Council of Nicaea (AD 325). In his gloss on the Athanasian doctrine that deification is the end of humanity, Professor John Macquarrie[1] makes the significant remark: 'To say that man is to be made God simply

[1] *God-Talk*, SCM Press, 1967, p. 139.

means that he is to realize the fulness of his being.' This position, though emerging from a different cultural background, is scarcely distinguishable from that of the Hindu Vedanta, which holds that a state of non-duality between God and man can be intuitively experienced.[1] At this level it is at least arguable that Catholicism, the most highly evolved form of Hinduism, and Mahayana Buddhism are variations on a single theme. In more precise Christian terminology, we have here the unpreachable experience of St Paul: 'It is no longer I who live, but Christ who lives in me' (Galatians 2.20).

The experience of sharing in the divine nature (cf. 2 Peter 1.4), though incapable of being verbalised, was in fact held out as a prospect in the teaching of the early Church— as Adolph Harnack, despite his Lutheran antipathy to the doctrine, is compelled by his integrity as an historian to admit:

> The supreme message of Christianity was its promise of this divine state to every believer. We know how, in that age of the twilight of the gods, all human hopes concentrated upon this aim, and consequently a religion which not only taught but realized this apotheosis of human nature (especially in a form so complete that it did not exclude even the flesh) was bound to have an enormous success. . . . Even after the great epoch when 'gnosticism' was opposed and assimilated, the church went forward in the full assurance that she understood and preached apotheosis as the distinctive product of the Christian religion.[2]

Lest all this should seem to suggest too grandiose notions of human destiny, let us linger for a moment over the Johannine

[1] See my *The End of Religion*, pp. 110–111.
[2] Harnack, *Mission and Expansion of Christianity*, London and New York, 1908, vol. i, pp. 238–239. Quoted from Alan Watts, *Behold the Spirit*, Random House, New York, 1947 and 1971. From the standpoint of a Catholic Christian, this is perhaps the most stimulating and worthwhile of the late Alan Watts's many books. On the passage quoted he comments shrewdly: 'Harnack, as a liberal Protestant regarding the Johannine literature alien to the actual teaching of Christ, was naturally unable to recognize this as the original essence of the Gospel.' *Ibid.*, p. 251.

theology. In John 10.30, Jesus, confronted by a crowd attending the feast of the Dedication at the Jerusalem Temple, makes the extraordinary claim: 'I and the Father are one.' At this his hearers prepare to stone him. He then says: 'I have shown you many good works from the Father; for which of these do you stone me?' To which they reply: 'We stone you for no good work but for blasphemy; because you, being a man, make yourself God.' Jesus does not withdraw his claim but says something which is intended to place it in focus: 'Is it not written in your law, "I said, you are gods" (*Psalm* 82.6)? If he called them gods to whom the word of God came (and scripture cannot be broken), do you say of him whom the Father consecrated and sent into the world, "You are blaspheming", because I said, "I am a son of God".' [The Greek original does not have '*the* Son of God'.]

In other words, Jesus is saying that his sonship is a gift of the Father, a special relationship in view of his saving mission to the world, while at the same time it is paralleled by that of the persons addressed in the Psalm referred to as 'gods' and 'sons of the Most High'. The use of the phrase 'sons of God' elsewhere in the Old Testament—e.g., Genesis 6.2; Job 1.6; 38.7—supports the view that, within the present context, Jesus is regarding himself as of the company of the men of the past who were considered to have partaken of the divine nature. Where Jesus' sonship is unique is not with reference to his humanity but with respect to his eternal generation by the Father as the second person of the Holy Trinity. Here he is the Logos, the Word which actually is God (John 1.1), which now divinizes our human nature. Consequently everything that can be said of God can likewise be said of Christ as the Logos, and everything that can be said of humanity can be said of Jesus the man—even to the point of his being involved, though sinless, in sin (2 Corinthians 5.21).

Enough has been noted up to this point to throw doubt on the widespread Christian assumption that, whatever current religious controversies may be about, at least the basic questions concerning God and Jesus Christ have finally been settled. On the contrary: without questioning the validity of ancient doctrinal formulas, we should remind ourselves that they are of necessity inadequate. At the Council of Nicaea, where the Christology we have just outlined was officially formulated, those chiefly concerned admitted that what they were trying to express was really inexpressible. They used the terminology available to them and attempted to pinpoint the Incarnation with such words as 'substance' and 'essence'. The difficulty of applying ordinary human speech to the transcendent Deity had always been there. Many of the Old Testament notions of God, as an autocratic despot, benevolent or otherwise, which are still echoed in the Church's liturgy, may derive from all too human sources. It was possibly Akhenaten (Amenhotep IV, fourteenth century BC), Pharaoh of Egypt, as Freud suggests, who focused Moses' attention on the idea of monotheism. We know that the veneration of God as 'King of kings and Lord of lords' borrows the official title of the Persian emperors. Under the great prophets, particularly Jeremiah, the relation between God and man becomes more human, even tender; until with Jesus God is unequivocally Father and we are his children, so establishing an affinity between Creator and creature. But Jesus himself, at the end of his life, may have been compelled in his extremity to abandon all positive concepts of God.[1] Whether later notions of the Godhead evolved in the minds of metaphysicians, mystics and scientists are more illuminating probably depends on the individual's point of view: St Thomas's 'subsistent being', or the more modern 'ground of being' or 'ultimate reality', have at least the advantage of largely eliminating anthropomorphic conceptions from the

[1] See p. 66.

Absolute. More helpful perhaps is an attempted harmonisation with contemporary physics, which seems to preserve both God's power and his personality, but is likely to be resisted by those who cannot distinguish the reality of the divine immanence from pantheism: the idea of God 'as the total energy-field of the universe, including both its positive and negative aspects, in which the whole is expressed in or implied by every part or process, as is the brain in each one of its cells'.

Terminology is fortunately free and theists obviously should think about God in ways they find most helpful. However it is well to remember that faith is not adherence to a form of words but an openness and trusting attitude to truth and reality, whatever it may turn out to be. It was just this that was required of those who were to accept Jesus. He had explicitly warned his critics against mental rigidity. 'You search the scriptures, because you *think* that in them you have eternal life . . .' (John 5.39); though in fact, rightly understood, they do testify to Christ. Christians are unlikely to be led into idolatry by images of wood and stone, but they could be by words and ideas—which are no more than mental images of God. Awareness of this situation is rather more than implied in the tradition of Catholic thought outlined earlier in these pages, as it is in those aspects of eastern religion which we are now to consider. Constructively we find the Second Vatican Council urging, by way of witness to genuine Christianity, 'dialogue and collaboration with the followers of other religions'. We are encouraged to 'acknowledge, preserve and promote' whatever spiritual and moral goodness is to be found there, as well as the values of their social and cultural setting.

The following passage from the Council's *Declaration on the Relationship of the Church to Non-Christian Religions* deserves quotation in full:

> For all peoples comprise a single community, and have a single origin, since God made the whole race of men dwell

over the entire face of the earth (cf. Acts 17.26). One also is their final goal: God, his providence, his manifestations of goodness, and his saving designs extend to all men (cf. Wis. 8.1; Acts 14.17; Rom. 2.6, 7; 1 Tim. 2.4) against the day when the elect will be united in 'that Holy City' ablaze with the splendour of God, where the nations will walk in his light (cf. Apoc. 21.23f.). . . .

Thus in Hinduism men contemplate the divine mystery and express it through an unspent fruitfulness of myths and through searching philosophical inquiry. They seek release from the anguish of our condition through ascetical practices or deep meditation or a loving, trusting flight towards God.

Buddhism in its multiple forms acknowledges the radical insufficiency of this shifting world. It teaches a path by which men, in a devout and confident spirit, can either reach a state of absolute freedom or attain supreme enlightenment by their own efforts or by higher assistance.[1]

Despite this authoritative encouragement, a difficulty may suggest itself to the Christian reader. Even the most casual student is aware that Hinduism is a theistic religion. Indeed he may think that trouble arises because it has a multiplicity of gods—though in fact they are all reducible to, are manifestations of, the One.[2] But such is not the case with Buddhism, which has even been described as 'atheistic'. It is true that the Buddha broke with the Brahmin priesthood, criticising its elaborate system of worship and over-subtle speculations. He was concerned with a way, not a theory, of living, and this led him to discourage by silence those who asked questions about the existence of a supreme being or the soul's immortality. Nonetheless, that his teaching implied an uncreated reality beyond the reach of the senses is undeniable. One of the earliest and best known texts in the Buddhist scriptures is the following:

There is an unborn, unoriginated, uncreated, unformed. Were there not this unborn, unoriginated, uncreated, unformed,

[1] Translations from *The Documents of Vatican II*. Edited by Walter M. Abbott, S.J. Copyright 1966 by the America Press, pp. 660–663.
[2] See the author's *The End of Religion*, p. 116.

there would be no escape from the world of the born,
originated, created, formed.—*Udana*, viii, 3.

The so-called Buddhist atheism has been neatly situated by
Dom Bede Griffiths:

> As regards Buddhism, it is true that the Buddhist does not
> believe in 'God', but he does believe in an infinite, eternal,
> transcendent Reality, which is characterized by wisdom and
> compassion, and what else do we mean by 'God'?[1]

Christianity depends in practice on our making meaningful
the three concepts of 'God', 'love' and 'neighbour'. Let us
glance at one or two related ideas in the Hindu-Buddhist
tradition.

The Hindu-Buddhist tradition

In the first place it is noteworthy that where Christians
talk about 'love', Hindus and Buddhists speak of *karuna*—
'active compassion'. Unfortunately, for us in the West,
'compassion' is almost as tired and overworked a word as
'love' itself. In Indian religion, compassion is linked with
'wisdom' (*prajna*), which bears the sense not so much of
cumulative understanding as of the ultimate intuition.
Wisdom so considered, when brought into action, is in fact
indistinguishable from compassion. Only when the mind is
cleared of self-concern—in the form of ignorance, delusion,
craving and aversion—can one have genuine sympathy, or
better, *empathy*, with others. Accordingly, Hindu and Buddhist scriptures, focusing on what is primary, have more to
say of wisdom than directly of compassion. Good intentions
are not enough; one must react to the situation as it truly is,
all misunderstanding eliminated. For the Hindu, God is the
source of this wisdom-compassion which he gives to us,
destroying our ignorance. Only by being united to him
through meditation can we practise compassion. So Krishna

[1] A letter in *The Tablet* 7 July 1973.

(an avatar of the Deity) addresses Arjuna in the *Bhavagad Gita* (10.8–11):

> I am the One source of all: the evolution of all comes from me. The wise think this and they worship me in adoration of love.
> Their thoughts are on me, their life is in me, and they give light to each other. For ever they speak of my glory; and they find peace and joy.
> To those who are ever in harmony, and who worship me with their love, I give the Yoga of vision and with this they come to me.
> In my mercy I dwell in their hearts and I dispel their darkness of ignorance by the light of the lamp of wisdom.[1]

Buddhism considers *mahakaruna*, 'great compassion' to be identical with 'Buddha-nature'. The *Nirvana Sutra* tells us: 'Great compassion and a great pitying heart is called Buddhanature.' In more practical terms;

> Gifts are great, the founding of temples is meritorious, meditation and religious exercises pacify the heart, comprehension of the truth leads to Nirvana—but greater than all is loving-kindness (*karuna*). As the light of the moon is sixteen times stronger than the light of all the stars, so is loving-kindness sixteen times more efficacious in liberating the heart than all other religious accomplishments taken together. This state of heart is the best in the world. Let a man remain steadfast in it while he is awake, whether he is standing, walking, sitting, or lying down.[2]

Buddhists think of the appropriate attitude towards what the New Testament calls 'neighbour' as one of *friendliness* (*metta*) but here neighbour includes along with human beings the whole of the animate creation. 'Mindfulness of friendliness' is a theme for meditation. It is believed that the waves of friendliness poured out by many thousands of meditating monks have a very positive effect on the welfare of the world. These are the good 'vibes' (= vibrations) which

---

[1] From the translation by Juan Mascaró, Penguin Books, 1962, pp. 84–85.
[2] *Sayings of Buddha*, Peter Pauper Press, Mt Vernon, New York. 1957, p. 12.

perceptive young people expect to feel when in the presence
of anyone supposedly religious. On the following lines,
seemingly spontaneous in their simplicity, from a Discourse
in the Buddhist canon of scripture, it would be superfluous
to comment:

> May all be happy and safe!
> May all beings gain inner joy—
> All living beings whatever
> Without exception, weak or strong,
> Whether long or high
> Middling or small, subtle or gross,
> Seen or unseen,
> Dwelling afar or near,
> Born or yet unborn—
> May all beings gain inner joy.
> May no being deceive another,
> Desire another's sorrow.
>
> As a mother cares for her son,
> Her only son, all her days,
> So towards all things living
> A man's mind should be all-embracing.
> Friendliness for the whole world,
> All-embracing, he should raise in his mind,
> Above, below, and across,
> Unhindered, free from hate and ill-will.[1]

Hinduism and Buddhism, like Christianity, have their
forms of popular worship. Devotion to Vishnu (his best
known avatars being Krishna and Rama) and Shiva can be
observed in cities and villages all over India. For Buddhists
of the Pure Land school Amitabha (in Japan, Amida), the
Buddha of Infinite Light, is the intermediary between
Supreme Reality and mankind; faith in him ensures rebirth
in his western paradise. But the Hindu while engaged in
chanting and ceremonies has a sense, more vivid than that

[1] Quoted from *The Buddhist Tradition*, edited by Wm Theodore de Bary, The
Modern Library, New York, 1969, pp. 37–38.

normally suggested by Christian worship, that the externals of religion, though helpful no doubt, are in the final analysis illusory: veils which both manifest and hide that which lies beyond them. Similarly, the inner significance of Amitabha is the true or higher 'self', and rebirth into his paradise is the supreme 'enlightenment' for the welfare of all.

Meditation and Buddhism

The aspect of Buddhism which may prove most rewarding for Christians to examine, and possibly incorporate in their own devotional life, is the technique of meditation—which is perhaps nearer to what Catholic spiritual writers describe as contemplation, since the mental activity involved is intuitive rather than discursive. Elsewhere can be found some relevant observations by the present writer on this topic[1] and in a later chapter[2] we shall attempt briefly to survey its background at a deeper level. Here we shall place the Buddhist psychology conveniently within a Christian setting. It seems possible to do this by way of a simple commentary, as distinct from scholarly exegesis, on a text from the Sermon on the Mount: 'Blessed are the pure in heart, for they shall see God' (Matthew 5.8).

The heart in Hebrew psychology is the seat of thought and will rather than of emotion. The pure heart, we may therefore say, is one in which the 'citadel of the mind' (a Buddhist phrase) has been cleansed and the will stabilised. When this state is reached, according to the Hindu-Buddhist tradition, God is already present within the human consciousness: though not as a direct vision, since God cannot be involved in a knowing-subject versus known-object relationship—any more than, to employ the analogies of Indian theology, fire can burn itself or water can wet itself. In other words, what is promised to the pure in heart does not come as a subsequent reward—which is probably its Christian eschatological

[1] See *The End of Religion*, pp. 227-232.   [2] Chapter 5.

meaning—but is the other side of the coin, the complement, of the purity itself. Bring the mind into the requisite condition, and God who is already there as the divine 'ground' of our being, is blissfully *realised*. So understood, meditation is not a search for, or even a finding of God; it is an enlightened awareness of the realities of our situation.

From this it follows that the contemplative activity we are now discussing is something distinct from what Christians normally mean by 'prayer'. The point is important since prayer—whether of petition, adoration or thanksgiving—for all its importance in the life of a Christian, can sometimes be used as a spiritual labour-saving device. We present our mental state to God and expect him to acknowledge and perhaps do something about it; whereas under his beneficent power, which we could not escape if we tried, we should be exercising to the full our own insight and effort. The Christian theological principle operative here is not the Pelagian superfluousness of divine grace, but the truth that the First Cause does not normally by-pass secondary causes: the simple axiom that God helps (perhaps *only* helps!) those who help themselves. For this reason, incidentally, perceptive persons are apt to cast a questioning eye on official announcements of days of prayer in this or that public calamity—that strife might cease or a conflict be averted, for example. More interesting would be the disclosure of what those responsible or immediately concerned are actually doing to avert the avowed crisis. 'All men desire peace,' wrote the author of the *Imitation of Christ*, 'but few desire the things that make for peace.' Throughout history statesmen have been ready to urge the populace to appeal to the immortal gods for aid in a worthy cause, while pursuing privately their own not so worthy designs. Gibbon laid his sceptical finger on the nub of the problem: a willingness to use religion as a means to an end. 'The various modes of worship, which prevailed in the Roman world, were all considered by the people to be equally true; by the philosophers, as equally false; and by the magistrates, as equally useful.'

These seeming irrelevancies are worth mentioning because the form of contemplative meditation we are now considering is not an other-worldly flight from the realities of the human condition. Rather it is a confrontation with them, a path of truth-seeking reaching beyond the words and forms of conventional religion. Since thought is tied to language, and inner attitudes are linked with external acts, the meditator will usually be helped by employing as a background the familiar practices of his religion. What he needs to understand, however, is that God cannot be placed before his mind as an object to be thought about or directly contemplated. On the contrary, his mind needs to be brought into such a condition that God, who is already present there, becomes a conscious reality. This is what Buddhists mean by knowing the 'Buddha nature' and how Christian saints have understood the saying that 'the kingdom of God is within you'.

Contemplative meditation calls at times for silence and solitude, but it does not in itself demand a withdrawal from, still less a contempt for, the world and its ways. They should be seen for what they are. Buddhism holds that the world we see is not a multiplicity of separate entities, but a chain of existence, a moving panorama in which nothing is permanent or stable. Daily life is made up of a series of transitory happenings. Recognising them as such—which is difficult, since we tend to give substance to what is unsubstantial—we have the opportunity to grow in wisdom and compassion. Does this view really differ from that taught by St Paul who seems to have held, like the Buddha, that suffering arises from ignorance of our true situation? 'For this slight momentary affliction is preparing for us an eternal weight of glory beyond all comparison, because we look not to the things that are seen but to the things that are unseen; for the things that are seen are transient, but the things that are unseen are eternal' (2 Corinthians 4.17, 18).

Some lines from the poet Tennyson may set the mood for a closer examination of what is involved in contemplative meditation:

> I am a part of all that I have met;
> Yet all experience is an arch wherethro'
> Gleams that untravell'd world, whose margin fades
> For ever and for ever when I move.

When I move. . . ! The point of meditation, or rather its condition, is not to move: to stop the movement of the mind, and even, for a time, movements of the body. 'Be still, and know that I am God' (Psalm 46.10). Movement implies change, a going to or away from somewhere, an achieving or abandoning of something. The practice of meditation, until it becomes habitual, requires stillness and if possible quietness, but the state which it engenders carries over into our everyday occupations, which will doubtless be full of movement. What are the movements of the mind that need to be stilled? They are not merely the surface distractions by which most people are bothered when they try to meditate. These can be dispelled by so simple a device as quietly observing one's own breathing. Even passing thoughts may become translucent and so dissolved just by being noticed and then ignored. Although meditating is not praying, an ancient Catholic description of prayer is here wholly applicable: the opening of the mind and heart to God. To God both in his height and in his fulness; that is to say, awareness of the divine presence at the apex, so to speak, of the human spirit, but also in the world around us. For this reason it is often more helpful to keep the eyes open rather than shut during meditation. 'The unenlightened man eschews phenomena but not thought,' writes a Zen master. 'The enlightened man eschews thought but not phenomena.'

In the contemplative state the mind is both empty and full.

It is empty of thought, ideas and images, yet full of awareness. This paradoxical condition has led Christians who have
experienced it to speak of 'darkness luminously bright', or
like St John of the Cross, of 'the night more lovely than the
dawn'. Buddhist authorities are more down-to-earth; they
regard mindfulness, awareness, as the heart of religion; it is
not a mystical transport but the mind in its true state, matter
of fact—the supreme fact. A Buddhist saint, Shantideva,
writes as follows:

> For those desiring to protect the mind, I fold my hands in
> prayer: With all zeal protect both mindfulness and total
> awareness. When practised by the mind without total aware-
> ness, instruction and reflection escape from mindfulness like
> water from a leaking jar. Many who have been instructed,
> who are faithful and intent upon zeal, become sinful and
> impure because of a lack of awareness.[1]

The Hindu-Buddhist tradition perhaps teaches more
clearly than the Christian that the only place we can com-
mune with God is here and the only time we can do so is
now. Though the Bible has a helpful reminder: 'A man of
understanding sets his face toward wisdom, but the eyes of
a fool are on the ends of the earth' (Proverbs 17.24). The
importance of the here-and-now was well understood by such
Catholic masters of the spiritual life as St François de Sales
and Père de Caussade, but the point may have been obscured by Christianity's over-valuation of history, its concern
for what literally happened or could yet happen. Assimilating the lessons of the past and intelligently anticipating the
future are clearly a part of practical every-day living, but
these mental activities lie on the circumference of religion
not at its centre. Of all attempts to make the Church more
'relevant', speculations about the future are probably the most
sterile. The eschatological passages in the New Testament

[1] Quoted from Marion L. Matics, *Entering the Path of Enlightenment*, Macmillan Company, New York, 1970, p. 164.

spring from their time and place, particular not general, and are therefore to be understood figuratively. Christian hope, instead of being focused on some visionary millennium, finds its truest expression in the confident outburst of St Paul: 'For I am sure that neither death nor life, . . . not things present, nor things to come, . . . nor anything else in all creation, will be able to separate us from the love of God in Christ Jesus our Lord' (Romans 8.38, 39).

Christians who practise contemplative meditation may learn by experience that their own religion, no less than those of the East, is concerned with the 'eternal now'—that which St Augustine called the *nunc stans*. 'Behold, now is the acceptable time, now is the day of salvation' (2 Corinthians 6.2). Or in the simple direct language of the Lord himself: 'Therefore do not be anxious about tomorrow, for tomorrow will be anxious for itself' (Matthew 6.34). The movements of the mind, from which we can withdraw during meditation, are precisely those that take us away from the present moment. Buddhism is at its strongest in its convincing account of what these are; their source is psychosomatic, lying at a much deeper level than the mental ripples we call distractions. They are: delusion, craving and aversion.

Delusion means that we are self-deceived: we fail to understand ourselves and consequently do not grasp the situation in which we are. The root of the trouble is a preoccupation, possibly quite unconscious (thereby increasing the delusion!), with our own ego. We strive to protect it from attack or enhance it in the eyes of others: which makes us defensive or aggressive by turns. We think we are misunderstood: whereas, as often as not, it is we who misunderstand. We may be living in a little world of our own—and prefer it that way, since it appears cosier and more comfortable than the seemingly bleak world of actual life. Or we may have 'ideals' (a rich source of delusion) so precious to us that we refuse to submit them to critical scrutiny. Instead, we strive to put them into immediate effect, perhaps impose them upon others, forgetful that often 'the best is the enemy of the good'. In any area of life that concerns us, not knowing, not wanting to know, indicates that we are deluded. In the field of religion, not to distinguish between the symbol and the symbolized, the verbal formula and what it points to, is to cloud the mind with one of the most baneful forms of delusion.

Craving for persons, which is lust, or for things, which is greed, are too familiar to call for much elucidation. The problem arises when normal human desire is carried to excess so that it becomes obsessive. Overweening ambition is a conspicuous example, but wishful thinking under any of its aspects exemplifies it in some degree. Unreasonable discontent with the work we have to do, or the place where we are, or the people we are obliged to associate with, are negative forms of craving. We long for the situation to be otherwise. The same can be said of unjust favouritism and exercising arbitrary preferences. St François de Sales was to reach a point when he could say: 'I have hardly any desires, but if I were to be born again I should have none at all. We should ask nothing and refuse nothing, but leave ourselves in the arms of divine Providence without wasting time in any desire, except to will what God wills of us.'

Aversion is no less self-explanatory than craving. It is a turning away in distaste from what displeases us. Hatred, envy and jealousy are obvious forms of it, which can lead directly to acts of violence and cruelty. Less conspicuously: shirking our responsibilities, declining to face situations or make decisions that duty requires of us, are forms of aversion, since they stem from dislike. Failure to summon up, when needed, the requisite amount of moral and physical courage, means that we are running away from something we should deal with courageously. Aversion, like craving, bears a kind of reciprocal relation to delusion: we crave and hate because we are deluded; we are deluded, therefore we crave and hate. Whether hatred is ever justifiable is a question we need not go into: a case could be made out for it from certain biblical texts. More to the point is a reminder from a Buddhist (which could also be a Christian) document, the *Dhammapada*, the 'Way of Righteousness':

> Never in this world is hate
> Appeased by hatred;
> It is only appeased by love—
> This is the eternal law.

Delusion, craving and aversion, the vicious circle in which we are all to some extent involved, are clearly elements of the human condition; we shall never be entirely rid of them. However, it is possible to withdraw from them for a while in the quiet of contemplative meditation. In this act of withdrawal we come nearer to our true selves and so nearer to God. 'Let me know myself', wrote St Augustine, 'let me know Thee.' When the mind is undeluded, craving for nothing, averting from nothing, then it is 'empty'—in the condition Zen people call *mu-shin*, which means no-mindness or no-thoughtness. It describes a state of awareness before the divison into duality—subject over against object—created by thought takes place. It brings with it the happiness attributed by the New Testament to those who are pure in heart (Matthew 5.8). Knowledge of the real is blissful—this fact of experience affords the surest grounds for confidence in God. We are here at the level where the Hindu-Buddhist tradition and Catholicism coincide.

Consider the doctrine of the Holy Trinity: to the Father can be appropriated the source of all being; to the Son, the Logos, belongs infinite consciousness; to the Spirit pertains the joy that flows from love without limit. 'To be', 'to know', 'to find joy', correspond to the *Sat-Cit-Ananda*: Being, Consciousness, Bliss of the Upanishads. This doctrine is echoed without variation, though in existential terms, in one of the aphorisms of St John of the Cross: 'In order to be All, do not desire to be anything. In order to know All, do not desire to know anything. In order to find the joy of All, do not desire to enjoy anything.' Nor need this experience—not a vision or an ecstasy but a deep-down sense of well-being— be limited to periods of meditation. With a sufficient degree of awareness, it could become a continuous state: we should then be living in the present. And the present is the only moment that really *is*: the point where time and eternity meet.

Liberation

The present moment is also the only point at which freedom can be realised. The lure of Eastern religion to so many, particularly among the young, is the prospect of liberation— freedom from bondage to sensuality, greed, hate, fear and self-centredness in all its forms. We in the West tend to think mostly of political and economic freedom: which is important, since satisfactory conditions in this respect, though not indispensable, can obviously be helpful not only to man's physical, but also to his spiritual well-being. For Indian religion the goal is interior freedom, liberation of the spirit: without any nostalgia for the past, fears about the present, or expectations for the future, one lives *now* on the spot where one is—since nostalgia, fear and expectation indicate the bondage of one's ego to the time-sequence. 'I have no hope, I have no fear, I am free'—were the words which the Greek poet Nikos Kazantzakis had inscribed on his tombstone. A fully enlightened Hindu or Buddhist would doubtless rejoice to be able to say the same.

To judge from its earliest documents, Christianity has nothing to learn from the East about the supreme value of freedom. Jesus came 'to set at liberty those who are oppressed' (Luke 4.18). If these words were at first understood to mean release from physical oppression, St Paul makes it clear that

it is the fearful 'spirit of slavery' that has been replaced by
the 'glorious liberty of the children of God' (Romans 8.21).
'Now the Lord is the Spirit, and where the Spirit of the Lord
is, there is freedom' (2 Corinthians 3.17). 'But he who is
united to the Lord becomes one spirit with him' (1 Corinthians 6.17). No words could declare more emphatically that
we attain true liberty by our spirit being united with God's
spirit. Yet what place does this teaching hold at the moment
in the Christian proclamation? The truth of course is that
freedom—even, perhaps especially, spiritual freedom—is an
acquired taste. People need to be taught to be free. Probably
the majority of the religiously-minded still prefer the seeming
security of submitting to the inevitable complexities of some
external authority, than to achieving 'a condition of complete
simplicity, costing not less than everything'. 'As the great
ocean has only one taste, the taste of salt', is a saying attributed to the Buddha, 'so my doctrine has only one flavour,
the flavour of liberation'. Would there be any danger of our
being misled if the Church, in both her teaching and
practice, were to season her message rather more plentifully
with that same unmistakable flavour?

4   Seeing Christianity anew

GIVEN LIBERTY, what place is left for authority and tradition —which, though operating differently, are as much a part of Eastern religion as they are of Christianity? The recognised spiritual master, guru or roshi, probably receives greater deference from his disciples than the average priest or minister. Catholic Christianity would cease to be itself were it to lose its nerve and, under contemporary pressures, fail to speak authoritatively of the tradition that has come down from Christ. Liberty without law degenerates into license. As has been well remarked, in the sphere of politics and economics, and perhaps also in religion, it is often the case that, 'As between the strong and the weak, it is liberty that oppresses and law that liberates'. The Church's central problem, then, is how to foster in her members the 'glorious liberty of the children of God' while exercising legitimate authority and preserving the authentic tradition. The solution surely lies, as has been discernible since Vatican II, in rendering the authority less obtrusive, transforming leadership into a ministry of service, while examining, and where necessary re-stating, the tradition in the light of all available knowledge. Both these activities are part of the art of persuasion; and when the individual is genuinely persuaded, his freedom is in no way curtailed.

The indwelling of the Spirit

Christianity needs to present itself, as far as possible, in such a manner that its truths are not historically or rationally 'proved', but rather self-proven in the light of experience. Though faith bears upon what is unseen, it carries with it its own assurance and conviction (cf. Hebrews 11.1). Earlier in these pages we have tried to face honestly the acknowledged limitations of the institutional Church; now it is time to consider the divine Spirit from which she derives her real life. The Fourth Gospel records how it was to the advantage of the earliest disciples that their Master's physical presence should be withdrawn, in order that, freed from the cult of even his personality, they might worship in spirit and truth (John 16.7; cf. 4.24). So, after the Resurrection, it came about. That the indwelling of the Spirit was for the early Christians not an abstract belief but a felt experience, cannot be doubted. No one can miss the sense of excitement conveyed by Acts and the Pauline letters. God had poured out his Spirit, the breath of life, source of wisdom and revelation (John 7.39; 20.22; Acts 2.16ff.; Hebrews 2.4). The individual Christian is a shrine of the Spirit, for he and his Lord are united as in a marriage (1 Corinthians 6.17–19), and a local church is a temple of the Spirit (3.16), a concept which in Ephesians (2.17–22) is applied to the Church as a whole. Moreover the Spirit brings the kind of freedom with which 'Christ has set us free' (Galatians 5.1). Love, joy, peace, patience, kindness, goodness, faithfulness, gentleness, self-control—these are the Spirit's 'fruit' (5.22). When they are present there is no need for any law.

In view of all this it is not surprising that there should be attempts in the Church today, both to recapture the sense of excitement produced by the Spirit's presence, and to test it by its fruits. For many people, group prayer and disposing oneself to the direct action of the Spirit, are a welcome alternative to what they feel to be the too impersonal character of the Church's regular worship. But here, I think, a caveat is called for, even though hardly needed by those who understand what they are about. Religious experience, symbolised in this case as an awareness of the Spirit's presence, cannot be self-generated; it is a pure gift. Can one be spontaneously prayerful when in a crowd or even a small group, each of whose members is engaged in a similar effort? Is there perhaps a hidden inconsistency: that of an individual trying to lose himself in God while at the same time unconsciously heightening his own self-consciousness? Possibly these are groundless misgivings. At any rate, it seems safe to say that Christian love shows itself most appealingly in an out-going warmth, person to person; it has nothing to do with collective emotionalism.

What is called for in religious worship is not impassivity but a 'centring' of the emotions; they are to be stimulated only in so far as they clarify rather than obscure true human insight. In his remarkable study *Mysticism East and West*, Rudolph Otto draws attention to the striking similarities between the teaching of the great Hindu theologian Shankara and the Catholic Meister Eckhart. Unknown to each other, widely separated in space and time, each in his own environment could have seen exemplified 'mysticism as an intoxicated eroticism', religious experience as 'excited emotionalism', the 'Krishna eroticism' of India paralleled by western 'bride mysticism'. Though the evidence points to Shankara and Eckhart alike having the deepest understanding of the spiritual life, God cannot for them be reached through the emotions; he is in the 'sphere of wonder'. Their outlook is 'cool, clear-sighted, serene and pure'.

Over-valuation of history

Attention has already been drawn to the insufficiency of approaching religion through the medium of 'that great dust-heap called "history"'. It is too often forgotten that, apart perhaps from an exhaustive factual chronicle, all history, even 'sacred' history, is a mental structure: an exercise in selectivity modified by preconceptions. More justly perhaps, because more subtly, the point has been made by Marcel Proust: 'The Muse which has gathered up all that the higher muses of philosophy and art have rejected, all that is not founded in truth, all that is only contingent but which reveals other laws, is what we call History.' The consequences of this situation are often better understood by Indian scholars than by their western colleagues, who tend to regard the appeal to history as not only relevant, which it is, but as decisive, which it is not. What actually happened, even if it could be determined is, in the context of religion, not nearly as important as the *meaning* of what happened. Indeed, the meaning, considered as a revelation, can sometimes dwarf into relative insignificance the external events which gave rise to it. The Pauline letters are proof of the validity of this principle at the very origins of Christianity. Thus today, when we recite the creed, we are not initially involved in any reminiscence about the past: 'I believe in God . . . and in Jesus Christ . . .'—*now*.

Seeing Christianity anew will certainly require purifying the language of religion and clarifying its meaning. The need is for a radical yet loving criticism (supportive and constructive) from within: such as Nagarjuna offered to Buddhism, Shankara to Hinduism, Thomas Aquinas to mediaeval Catholicism, a succession of major German theologians from Schleiermacher to Tillich to Protestantism. The results could reassure many among the vast numbers of the thoughtful yet uneasy faithful that Christianity has something more substantial to offer than an age-old ritual or a 'charismatic proclamation'. The Church could be shown as pointing more clearly to a path along which, even now, the immortal triad—the true, the good and the beautiful—is apprehensible. Linked with such a meditative practice as we have outlined in the previous chapter, this programme could rather more than suggest that the Christian revelation is not merely to be assented to but actually experienced, that the one who believes '*has* eternal life' (John 5.24).

In the sphere of human conduct the Church should appear as upholding something more significant than a code of conventional ethics, helpful as this may be. Religion and morality are by no means to be equated. The happiness promised in the Sermon on the Mount, or the invitation to follow St Paul's 'still more excellent way' (1 Corinthians 12.31ff.), raise the spirit above the precepts of good behaviour. At the level of moral striving we never really escape from well-intentioned egoism, more or less enlightened self-interest. The saint is protected from this illusion because, in the language of Hinduism, he 'covers himself with the truth of the universal self'.

East and West seem to meet in agreement on the point that there is a threefold path to God. First, there is the path of self-forgetting adoration, expressed in both private worship and in the Church's liturgy. Secondly, there is the path of selfless service of others, which finds expression in compassionate activity for the benefit both of the individual and society as a whole. Thirdly, there is the path of truth-realising experience, along which we are especially helped by contemplative meditation. According to temperament, we shall incline to one or other of these three ways—any one of which, selflessly pursued, can lead to conscious union with God. They are not mutually exclusive and each has its possibilities of abuse. The first can go astray into a mindless piety or an obsessive, even superstitious, preoccupation with rites and ceremonies. The second, sometimes endangered by an idealistic utopianism, can fail through a lack of practical wisdom: the eye to discern what, in any given context, is the truly helpful thing to do. The third, to which thinkers and intellectuals seem naturally drawn, can degenerate into an 'ego trip', the personal pursuit of contemplative bliss, with little regard to one's obligations to other people. However, awareness of these risks is the first step to overcoming them. Spiritually, even more than physically, we must be prepared to live dangerously, without any guarantee of security—except that of the Gospel: 'Whoever seeks to gain his life will lose it, but whoever loses his life will preserve it' (Luke 17.33).

Worship in spirit and truth

It is not often that a weekly congregation hears a sermon preached on such a text as: 'Yet the Most High does not dwell in houses made with hands' (Acts 7.48; cf. 17.24–28). Where he does dwell is within our own spirit: to know oneself truly as to draw near to God. 'If you are far from your own self,' asks St Augustine, 'how can you be close to God?' These are among the spiritual facts of life that today's Christians are most eager to hear about. 'Quite apart from the infusion of sanctifying grace God is already present to the soul by what the theologians call his ubiquity. He is there in the way in which he is present to everything he has made, giving to the soul its being and maintaining it in existence'.[1] This is the ontological foundation of the interior life, as our Lord himself is the model of how that life should be lived.

Jesus was the completely God-centred man; yet we seem to detect in his mind a deepening of his concept of God, until he transcends all concepts. Habitually he speaks of God as his Father; so, even in Gethsemane, he addresses him as 'Abba, Father' (Mark 14.36); but on the cross it is no longer Father, simply 'God'. It is '*My* God' (15.34) who appears to have deserted him. Dare we interpret this as meaning that Jesus, in his anguish, had been brought to the extreme point of abandoning any anthropomorphic notion of God? Many devout Jews of the period, as the late C. H. Dodd has pointed out, spoke of God as 'the One who really is', much

[1] Aelred Graham, *The Love of God*, Longmans, 1939. p. 207.

as some moderns speak of the 'ultimate reality', or the 'ground of being'. That something of this kind was the experience of the man Jesus would accord with the view of those theologians who maintain that in the depths of his spirit he at no time lost the awareness of God, whose content can never be conceptualised. If this were so, Jesus would have mentally broken through, without repudiating, all the concepts of God inherited from his Jewish tradition, to reach 'God as he is in himself' (as theologians were later to express it). He had passed in his own way through an ordeal far more terrible and self-denuding than St John of the Cross's 'dark night', to *realise* the goal of the individual self, self-absence—the Suffering Servant had been transformed into the Spirit, the Jesus of history become the mystical Christ. Do we catch here also an echo of the *neti, neti* ('not this, not this'—a reference to the self-manifesting Godhead, 'before whom words recoil') of the Upanishads, the *shunyata* (the *void*) of Buddhism?

In authentic Christianity there is a revolutionary element, but Christian renewal is not to be equated with revolution. If there is no continuity then it is not the Church that is being renewed but something else put in its place. Seeing Christianity anew means observing with discrimination how much of it, supposedly existing 'out there' is in part a projection of many minds, including perhaps one's own. If we are to interiorise the spiritual life, we must withdraw the projections and dissolve them in the light of a profound awareness. Here we could be helped if the Church's normal prayer life were supplemented by a form of meditation more common in the East than in the West. When life's fever is still, we can actually taste the atonement—the at-one-ment—between God and man.

Not even the 'I-Thou' relationship, in which the encounter or meeting with God is often described, does justice to the intimacy of the Johannine 'The glory which thou hast given

me I have given to them, that they may be one even as we
are one' (17.22). Neither 'contemplation' nor 'vision' seem to
catch the meaning; perhaps 'realisation' comes nearest: we
realise that Christ is our 'life' (Colossians 3.4). The subject-
object antithesis has been transcended, even though the
subjective self remains. 'Let me know myself', we have
recalled from St Augustine, 'let me know Thee'. Rudolf
Bultmann, in existential terminology, makes the same point:
'Man's life is moved by the search for God because it is
always moved, consciously or unconsciously, by the question
about his own personal existence. The question of God and
the question of myself are identical.'[1] In one way it is true to
say that God searches for us: he manifests himself to us as the
Self which we find when we no longer cling to the self-
conscious egos we call 'ourselves'. No effort or striving on our
part can bring about this divine manifestation: it is a response
to faith. And faith, ultimately, I think, is an awareness
beyond sense-perception that the power behind the universe
is not neutral, but gracious and beneficent, the unshakable
confidence that 'all shall be well and all manner of thing shall
be well'.

[1] Rudolf Bultmann, *Jesus Christ and Mythology*, SCM Press, 1960, p. 53.

5   Ultimate sharing

Opposed to any notion of mutual sharing is the concept of alienation. This is more than a fashionable word with Marxist and psychiatric overtones; it corresponds to a painful reality by which everyone is to some extent afflicted. To be exploited or merely used, to be compelled to perform inhuman, mechanical, unrewarding tasks yielding no intrinsic satisfaction, to be denied an adequate wage for one's work, to have no choice of livelihood except one that involves continual frustration—these are forms of alienation as it is commonly understood. They are symptoms of a deeper malaise: the lack of fellow-feeling of human beings with one another and a cleavage within the individual himself. Buddhists call this state of affairs *dukkha*, which is ordinarily translated as pain, suffering, ill, but which has the extended meaning of discomfort, frustration or disharmony with the environment. It is the *lacrimae rerum*, the tears that seem to flow from the very heart of things.

Religion may be regarded in practical terms as an attempt to deal with the problem of alienation. Its aim is to bring about a situation in which people are not strangers to one another—to actualise that one touch of nature which makes the whole world kin—or at odds with themselves. The second part of the problem is the more fundamental: remove the inner conflict within individuals and reciprocal good

fellowship is likely to follow. Disharmony within the self,
however, can only be put to rest in the light of genuine self-
knowledge—and this in its turn, or rather simultaneously, as
we have already noted, calls for a realisation of the supreme
Self, which we call God. But here the difficulty could be
increased: we may feel alienated from God himself, through
a sense of guilt and impotence. (Luther in his early years is
the classical example of this situation.) The danger is always
present so long as God is thought about in any positive
imagery, particularly that of much of the Old Testament,
still echoed in phrases from the Church's liturgy. The
solution lies in God incarnate, Christ, of whom we are now
brothers and sisters (cf. Romans 8.29), and specifically in his
'precious and very great promises', a pledge of the ultimate
sharing, that we should 'become partakers of the divine
nature' (2 Peter 1.4).

What is here being said was later formulated in a theology:
a doctrine of 'sanctifying grace', regarded as a quality super-
added to the soul. An Aristotelean category was substituted
for what the New Testament tells us—that we are concerned
with 'self-realisation' and 'participation in the very life of
God'.[1] To avoid a pantheistic interpretation some such
device was doubtless necessary, but it leaves us with an
impoverished notion of Christian spirituality, for which St
Paul provides a more satisfactory formulation: '. . . he who
is united to the Lord becomes one spirit with him' (1 Corinthians 6.17). Divine revelation is not something superimposed
upon the human condition but an elucidation of it. Thus we
can infer from a philosophical analysis that an infinite
Creator plus finite creation do not make two realities; the
latter is contained within the former in some indefinable
way. We exist more really in God than in ourselves. 'In him
we live and move and have our being' (Acts 17.28). To say

[1] See Alois Stöger, *The Second Epistle of Peter* in 'The Two Epistles of St Peter'.
Edited by John L. McKenzie, Burns & Oates, 1969, p. 136.

that we share in the divine nature, or that we are one spirit with the Lord, is to place humanity's situation within the context of the Incarnation, to shed upon it 'the true light that enlightens every man' (John 1.9).

Transcendent and immanent

Pantheism, like atheism, is one of those words which could usefully be kept out of serious religious discussion. In such statements as 'everything is God' or 'God does not exist', the key word 'God' is beyond definable meaning. To define anything we must state what category, or class of things, it belongs to and then add what differentiates it from other members of the same class. But this cannot be done with 'God', since he (to be literal, we could just as well say 'she', or even 'it'—as the mode of the divine personality is incomprehensible to us) does not belong to any class. This is one way of saying that God is transcendent; he transcends the categories. Accordingly theologians find it easier to say what God is not than what he is. Pantheism as a positive position therefore makes little sense; though we can certainly say that everything that exists is a manifestation of God—or in the words of the Psalmist: 'The heavens are telling the glory of God; and the firmament proclaims his handiwork' (Psalm 19.1). Atheism, on the other hand, being a negative word, could make quite a lot of sense, provided that what is denied is unworthy of the God of all goodness. Religion has in fact become more enlightened by the denial of false notions about God. Thus, as is so often the case, extremes meet: a pantheism which holds that everything we observe is divine coincides with a materialistic atheism based on the belief that what is observable is the only reality that exists.

Having made the point that God, considered as the Absolute, transcends all categories and cannot be conceptualised, we must at once criticise this position dialectically.

God is beyond 'name and form', the *reality* 'before which words recoil', and is therefore often spoken of by theologians negatively. When, however, we are confronted by such language as 'not this, not this' (*neti, neti*), 'emptiness' (*shunyata*), the 'void', it has to be understood that this negative terminology is itself to be negated. In other words, concepts and language, not the reality, of the Divine are what are being nullified. To put it succinctly, if a little technically, God is negated epistemologically but affirmed ontologically. Positive terms like *summum bonum*, truth, ultimate reality, are correctly applied to God, on the understanding that the manner in which such applications are realised is unknown to us. As the focus of faith and worship we cannot but think and speak of God positively. He is not emptiness but fulness— the *pleroma* (Ephesians 3.19 and elsewhere).

The terms transcendent and immanent as applied to God are spatial metaphors, to be understood with the provisos we have just been discussing. When engaged in worship or petitionary prayer we think of God objectively, when we 'find' God subjectively we do not *think* of him at all; we *realise* our true Self, we lose the sense of alienation and become authentic. As Berdyaev has pointed out, whatever is to be said of the material objects with which the physical sciences deal, spiritual reality is, so to speak, behind us in the life of the subject rather than spread out before us in the objective world. 'There is no greater mistake than to confuse objectivity with reality. The objective is that which is least real.' God's having become united, not with *a man* but with human nature (John 1.14), abolishes in this context the antithesis between subject and object, immanent and transcendent. Dietrich Bonhoeffer had right on his side when he criticised 'otherworldliness' and, in one of the profound intuitions of his *Sanctorum Communio*, wrote: 'Whoever happens to be one's neighbour and reachable is the transcendent.'

The mystical

We shall return to Bonhoeffer on a later page; for the moment let us pursue a line of thought which was hardly his. If God is *the* Reality, then it seems true to say that a person who does not find God everywhere, finds him truly nowhere. The word 'mystical' connotes in many minds what is out-of-this-world, vague and unreal; whereas our concern has been to try to elucidate what an age-long tradition, represented by both East and West, regards as the supremely *real*. Nevertheless we may welcome Wittgenstein's illuminating use of the term in his *Tractatus Logico-Philosophicus*: 'It is not *how* things are in the world that is mystical, but *that* it exists. To view the world *sub specie aeterni* is to view it as a whole—a limited whole. Feeling the world as a limited whole—it is this that is mystical' (Propositions 6.44 and 6.45). When 'from the timeless standpoint' we view the world as a limited whole, this carries with it implicitly a feeling of that by which the limited is judged to be such, i.e., the unlimited or unconditioned—that 'before which words recoil', to cite Shankara again, quoting the Upanishads. Here we find support in Wittgenstein's further statement: 'There are, indeed, things that cannot be put into words. They *make themselves manifest*. They are what is mystical' (6.522). Nor can the point that 'eternal life' is available *now* be better stated than it is by the same philosopher: 'If we take eternity to mean not infinite temporal duration, but timelessness, then eternal life belongs to those who live in the present' (6.4311).[1]

The mystic as here understood is the spiritual person par excellence; he lives in the light of what is perhaps the most luminous single statement in the Bible: 'God is spirit, and those who worship him must worship in spirit and truth' (John 4.24). Christian spirituality, being incarnational,

[1] The Wittgenstein quotations are taken from the translation of the *Tractatus* by D. F. Pears & B. F. McGuinness, Routlege & Kegan Paul, 1961.

embraces the flesh; it welcomes what is fully human, includes
the physical, the down-to-earth, the concrete, is opposed
only to a materialism which regards what can be perceived
by the senses as the sole reality. Thus the spiritual person will
live in the every-day world in a commonsense way—but with
a difference. The difference will lie in the *realisation* (not
simply the theoretical recognition) that egocentricity is the
root of the unspiritual: the spiritual is the universal. Here is
the end of the self-centred world of me and mine: 'Thy
kingdom come' means that my kingdom must go! The path
now lies open to mutual self-sharing. God shares himself with
us so that we may share ourselves with others.

The crown of the spiritual life, in terms of the Indian
tradition, is to achieve 'God-realisation'—that is, to be in a
state of awareness such that God is consciously *real*. The
God-realised or spiritual person (as in 1 Corinthians 6.17)
correspondingly has a sense of 'the mystical', as just now
described. Here there is sharing without any division: no
division within the self, no dividing oneself from others. The
internal conflicts between the outward appearance and the
inner reality, between the mask and the hidden thoughts and
feelings which it hides, between the various levels of the
personality, between the unconscious or subconscious on the
one hand and full consciousness on the other, are resolved.
The spiritual, the undivided person, whose eye is 'single'
(Matthew 6.22), is aware of his or her own motives and acts
honestly in the light of them, without self-deception or
deceiving others. The resulting air of coolness is not a pose, a
disguise for self-protection, or the lack of emotional demon-
strativeness an absence of feeling. In close interpersonal
relations, in love between friends, in sexual intimacies, as is
too obvious to need saying, the emotions will express themselves in all their vulnerability. But the general life-style of a
spiritually enlightened person will combine a compassionate
friendliness and involvement with a certain detachment and

serenity—a coincidence of seeming opposites: the secret of how 'to care and not to care'. The reason for this has already been given: the spiritual is the universal. Whence follow the disappearance of the egocentric outlook, the subordination of all private, parochial and sectional interests, the yielding of particular opinions and standpoints, in favour of a 'God's eye' view of the world, made possible by humanity's sharing in the divine nature.

Love without insight is blind, frustrating to the lover and the beloved alike. Wisdom without compassion operates only in the realm of theory. Buddhism teaches that wisdom, not as a philosophy but as deep intuition (*prajna*), and active compassion (*karuna*) are inseparable, two facets of one enlightened spiritual state. Our knowledge must be transmuted into self-giving love; for that, according to Christianity, is the way God acts. 'Your heavenly Father knows that you need . . .' (Matthew 6.32); 'For God so loved the world that he gave . . .' (John 3.16). We cannot see God as he is, but we can see him as embodied in the people around us; he realises himself in them just as he does in us. God does not look at the world as a lovable object outside himself, since nothing is outside himself. As the ultimate 'I'—'Before Abraham was, I am' (John 8.58)—he loves the world subjectively—in us. As with nature, so with love, we participate in his. 'No man has ever seen God; if we love one another, God abides in us and his love is perfected in us' (1 John 4.12). In this condition we are not egotistically separated off from anything or anyone. We can look at the world, not as impersonally isolated from it—judgementally perhaps, seeking to divide good from evil—but creatively, as God does: who 'makes his sun rise on the evil and on the good, and sends rain on the just and on the unjust' (Matthew 5.45).

6   On growing young

'THE PRESENT generation under the age of twenty-five is the wisest and holiest generation that the human race has ever seen. And by God, instead of lamenting, derogating, and imprisoning them, we should support them, listen to them and turn on with them.' One of those sweeping generalisations, we may say, that no one could possibly justify. Knowing its source, we can easily brush it aside. The words were spoken in a press interview by a specialist in psychedelic drugs, perhaps himself a casualty of his own experiments, an eccentric who like many of the unorthodox has been imprisoned and generally in trouble with the police, Dr Timothy Leary. Yet a related point is made more soberly in a similar context by Michael Schofield. When young people 'revolt against the conventional lives of older generations and proclaim their right to do their own thing, they are not thinking of an anarchic free-for-all. Their own thing is a meditative realization of their own senses and a greater awareness of their inner self.'[1] For the benefit of the conservative reader who finds these observations hard to swallow, an unimpeachable witness has given supporting testimony— Edmund Burke, in a letter to Fanny Burney, dated 29 July 1782: 'The arrogance of age must submit to be taught by youth.' More relevant today are the words of Brother

[1] Michael Schofield, *The Strange Case of Pot*, Penguin Books, 1971, p. 182.

Roger Schultz of the country monastery of Taizé: 'I would go to the ends of the earth to tell and tell again of my trust in the new generation.' (*Time*, 29 April 1974.)

There are few greater illusions than for an older person to suppose that he or she understands the young. To try to be one of them is perhaps an even graver mistake. Worth bearing in mind also is Hilaire Belloc's rather sour comment, that the easiest way to popularity is to flatter the young. Yet where, psychologically, a generation gap exists it is the old who are mostly to blame: they have the advantage over the youngsters of having been that way before them. When a boy or girl 'identifies' with an older person, the latter is not necessarily being regarded as a model to be imitated, or even as potentially an intimate friend, though such could turn out to be the case. Rather, he or she is one in whose company the young can be themselves, that is, find their own identity. For this to happen young people need to feel assured that the maturity to be looked for in the old has not obliterated the strengths and weaknesses of their own situation; in other words, that here humanity's childhood has flowered rather than faded. Today the seasoning and perspective that should come with age are still admired by the young—provided that they are not obtruded, but regarded as resources to be drawn upon in direct personal encounters, in which questioning and criticism must play their part.

Theodore Roszak, in his *The Making of a Counter-culture* comments shrewdly on the present, or at least recent, state of the younger generation. Observing that 'creative vision lies with the young', he complains that this can find little outlet under the conditions prevailing in modern western society. A highly developed and accelerating industrialism is causing young people to feel themselves trapped by the paternalism of a managerial expertise. They have either to become part of it or drop out altogether. Thanks to parental inadequacy too many adolescents find themselves 'stranded between a permissive childhood and an obnoxiously conformist adulthood'. Relief from this situation is often sought in religion, but there is not much evidence that the institutional Church is looked upon as meeting the need. In a society where Christianity's doctrinal and moral assumptions were agreed on and generally accepted, the Church could be a support amid the insecurities of youth. When, however, the whole concept of a structured Church is itself under challenge, and the quest is not for dogmatic religion but for self-transcending experience, it is not surprising that young people are looking elsewhere. As Bishop John A. T. Robinson has written:

> There is a revolt against the world we have to live in because it doesn't give life but death. Here as elsewhere there is a revolution of rising expectations. There is a quest on all sides for quality of life, expansion of consciousness and sensitivity, maturity of relationship, release of the human potential. The concern is for the exploration of inner space, of love, tenderness, togetherness, wholeness, the total environment of man.[1]

Becoming young

What then do we mean by older people, especially spokesmen for the Church, growing young? The qualities we associate with youth—unfortunately not in every case to be found there—are a willingness to learn and an outlook that is direct and simple. The first leads to an all round receptivity, the second to a desire to get behind what one sees so as to understand. Both these qualities tend, in most people, to diminish as they grow old. This is particularly apparent in the sphere of religion. Here the temptation is strong to stand by received opinions authoritatively delivered, without troubling to ask oneself what they mean or how much sense they make. Yet a faith that does not seek to understand is

[1] John A. T. Robinson, *The Difference in Being a Christian Today*, Collins Fontana Books, 1972, pp. 51–52.

hardly worth having—at least for those who believe that religion is concerned with a reality beyond the reach of physical science and academic philosophy. The majority of the young have an instinct that this must be so, if religion is to be taken seriously. But when they find that their elders can tell them little that they cannot tell themselves, that the thoughts they express and the advice they give are elementary and jejune, that the chief preoccupations of churchmen are law and order, ritual and ecclesiastical organisation, supplemented by vague generalities opposing sin and favouring virtue, then inevitably they turn elsewhere for a fresh vision of the true, the good and the beautiful, which is the proper nourishment of the human spirit at every age.

The physical arteries harden with age but those of the mind need not do so. When a person in his sixties loses touch, or is out of sympathy with those in their twenties, the danger signal is clear. So far as the rising generation is concerned, he is no longer in a learning situation. From this it follows that he is not in a position to hand on to those who come after him the Christian heritage he himself received. Having kept faith with it loyally but unthinkingly, never having faced any challenge to it, or enlarged and enriched it from the many available sources, he cannot present it to those who mental outlook, by age and upbringing, is different from his own. He is like the man in the Gospel who went and hid his one talent in the ground (Matthew 25.25). Churchmen still find it hard to reconcile themselves to the fact that the days of the doctrinal hand-out are over; religion must now be taught through a meeting of minds, sharing of experiences. This means a forgoing of status, the acceptance of person to person encounters, an opening of the mind to wider horizons, facing fundamental questions—not simply about Christianity and the Church, but about God and the world at large. For God so loved—not a just a nation, a chosen people, or even a church—but the world ('the cosmos'), as to send his Son,

the Logos of God, that those who accepted him might live,
enlightened by his enlightenment (cf. John 3.16; 8.12).

'Truly, truly, I say to you, unless one is born anew, he
cannot see the kingdom of God' (John 3.3). It would be
improper to take these words addressed to Nicodemus out of
their historic context. Nevertheless, many of the sayings in
the Fourth Gospel have, and were probably intended to have,
a universal as well as a particular reference. Some New
Testament scholars have seen these words as echoing Mark
10.15: '. . . whoever does not receive the kingdom of God
like a child shall not enter it.' To 'see' the kingdom is to
experience, to enjoy it. What is being spoken of is not a
return to childhood, but a second birth, from above, in the
power of God's Spirit. Without forcing the text we can surely
apply it to ourselves especially if, like Nicodemus, we have
any pretensions to being a 'teacher of Israel'. Conversion, in
the sense of turning back and having second thoughts, a
change of heart, with all that this implies in terms of awareness and self-criticism, is bound up with genuine religious
practice: ' . . . unless you turn and become like children, you
will never enter the kingdom of heaven' (Matthew 18.3).
Obviously this is not an invitation to childishness, but to
reawaken the capacity to learn, to be receptive, to look at the
Christian truths, not as ossified in familiar verbal formulas,
but as if we were seeing them for the first time.

At the time of Vatican Council II there was much talk of
Christian 'renewal'. It was hardly noticed then, though it
has since become apparent, that Church structures and
institutions cannot, strictly speaking, be renewed; they can
only be changed, with the inevitable risk that the change
may be for the worse. The recurring cycle of the seasons:
birth, blossoming fruitfulness, decay and death, in which our
bodies no less than the rest of nature are involved, points to
the radical impermanence of the human condition. The
man-made factors in the Church's institutional structure,

and they are many, share the instability of the power that
brought them into being. They could collapse, perhaps they
are already collapsing: an entirely new cycle of the Church's
existence may be imminent. Christians become young again,
born anew in the Spirit, by sitting lightly to religion's
external supports, trusting confidently in God but cherishing
few expectations. 'The wind (i.e., *pneuma* = spirit) blows
where it wills, and you hear the sound of it, but you do not
know whence it comes or whither it goes; so it is with everyone who is born of the Spirit' (John 3.8). For all practical
purposes, God speaks to us not in the past or future, but now.
'So we do not lose heart. Though our outer nature is wasting
away, our inner nature is being renewed every day' (2 Corinthians 4.16).

The youthful Jesus

Much stress has been laid in the preceding pages on Jesus
as the incarnate Word, the Logos of God, a manifestation in
human form of ultimate reality, the ground of all that exists.
Of no less interest is his appearance as man, working and
teaching and finally dying in Roman-occupied first-century
Palestine. Within these limits of space and time he manifested the fulness of the Godhead, to the extent that it could
be revealed in a single human body (Colossians 2.9). Further-
more he was a young man, his career being over at latest in
his early thirties. As C. H. Dodd, with the majority of New
Testament scholars, has insisted, Jesus is to be placed firmly
'on the field of history, and in relation to real problems arising
out of human nature and society as they are'. Was he in any
sense a rebel—a role in which many of today's younger
generation like to see him? He was certainly a radical, in the
sense that he reached to the roots of the complex religious
situation of his day. Even though Jesus' mission was to form
a revitalised 'people of God', not to encourage directly
Jewish national aspirations, it is not altogether surprising

that many who listened to him misunderstood his message.

The Gospel accounts make it clear that his campaign in
Galilee had been conducted with such vigour and initial
success that he could command the attention, in the sight
of anyone who cared to look on, of four or five thousand
followers at a time. 'Perceiving that they were about to come
and take him by force to make him king, Jesus withdrew
again to the hills by himself' (John 6.15). In this brief phrase,
as Dodd has pointed out, the Fourth Gospel passes over what
must have been a gravely critical situation. It was no less
than an attempted rising against the government with Jesus
as leader. When the end came at Jerusalem, whatever may
have been the precise charge brought against him by his
Jewish compatriots, the alleged crime for which he was
unjustly executed by Pilate was sedition: as 'King of the
Jews', he had been identified as in rebellion against Caesar.
This is what contributes to make Jesus such an admired figure
in the eyes of many of the young: he forced a confrontation
with both the religious and political 'establishments', he testi-
fied to the truth as he saw it and died for what he believed.

It may not be too fanciful to hope that, when ecclesiastical
life becomes less tension-laden and more enlightened, the
Church will institute a feast in honour of the youthfulness of
Christ. Such a celebration would have at least as much
relevance to the human condition, as it presents itself today,
as that of his kingship. The emphasis, needless to say, would
not be on the glorification of youth—as if there were something desirable about being *puer aeternus*, an adolescent
refusing to grow up. Rather we should be reminded that our
salvation was achieved by one in his early manhood, and so
invited to keep our mental eyes unclouded, our hearts open
and responsive, thus carrying youth's most-to-be-treasured
characteristics through to old age. The dull, grey, heavy
men that the young of today find so unappealing, are not

simply those who have grown physically old—since life-experience and genuine maturity were never more sought after by the young—but those who themselves, even at an early age, failed to develop the openness and spontaneity of youth, or who, advancing in years, have allowed their mental arteries to harden, who tend to regard all that is new as bad news and every change as a change for the worse.

The younger clergy

In parenthesis, it is worth taking a glance at differences of outlook between the old and the young among the Catholic clergy. A report from the Federal German Republic, based on a careful survey, shows a gulf between the older and younger clergy covering most aspects of a priest's relationship to his calling.[1] Asked what gave them most spiritual help, 75 per cent of priests ordained between 1936 and 1940 answered 'celebration of the liturgy', while of those ordained between 1966 and 1970 only 55 per cent placed the sacraments in first place. About spiritual retreats: among the pre-1921–1925 generation, 41 per cent claimed to be helped by them, but they decrease in popularity until only 14 per cent of the latest intake are enthusiastic. As for religious instruction as a regular part of the school curriculum, 82 per cent of those ordained before 1931 approved, while only 35 per cent of the 1961–1970 age group agree, and they would prefer to see religion become a voluntary subject for the fourteens and over. A disparity of view between clergy and laity appears on a particularly interesting point: while 75 per cent of the active secular priesthood consider preaching to be of paramount importance, only 47 per cent of the laity go along with this—a fact of which the homily-addicted members of the cloth should surely take note! Again, while a fairly high proportion of young priests believe that they should live at a

[1] See 'Priests in conflict', an account by Stella Musulin, *The Tablet*. 10 November 1973.

standard lower than the average in their community, a majority among the laity think that they should live on an equal footing.

These statistics (concerning 20,055 members of the clergy, of which 89 per cent were secular priests and 11 per cent religious) come only from West Germany and to what extent they could be paralleled by those drawn from Britain and the United States is a matter for conjecture, though there is evidence to suggest that a corresponding situation exists in both these countries. Among the youngest age group, in West Germany at least, only 4 per cent are entirely at peace with the institutional Church. On the highly controversial issue of celibacy, a priest who is opposed to it does not necessarily wish to marry. He may personally approve of celibacy: what he is against is its enforcement through the vertical, authoritarian structure of the hierarchy. It is his concept of personal freedom which is involved. The trend among the younger clergy to adapt to the society in which they live is unmistakable. The urge to serve humanity is not seen as a form of ascetic practice—an embracing of personal poverty, for example. It coexists with a felt need for sufficient comfort and companionship. But the fact is inescapable: the younger the priest, the more he finds his principal source of strength in the service of others. At the same time there is developing a vital interest in, and desire to practise some form of meditative prayer, since the fuel required for continuous self-giving comes only from the deeper resources of the spirit.

A young theologian: Dietrich Bonhoeffer

Evidence of the religious situation in West Germany, with its emphasis on a Christianity that is socially and even politically orientated, inevitably calls to mind the life-work of one of the outstanding personalities of this century, Dietrich Bonhoeffer. Born in Breslau, 4 February 1906, he was executed in a concentration camp, April 1945, on account of his involvement in a plot to overthrow the Nazi regime. Well described by his biographer Eberhard Bethge, as 'Man of Vision—Man of Courage', Bonhoeffer, though not a systematic theologian, left behind him an important theological legacy which cannot be ignored by those concerned to discover Christian truth. Like Kierkegaard, whom in some ways he resembles, he propounded his thought in original and striking phrases, whose meaning it is not always easy to determine. 'Religionless Christianity', Jesus as 'the man for others', 'world come of age', the neighbour who is reachable as 'the transcendent'—these are the themes being discussed, not only in divinity schools and seminaries, but wherever thoughtful young people gather together to talk about religion.

The quotation which appears as the epigraph of this book is taken from one of Bonhoeffer's letters to his future biographer, dated 30 April 1944, written from his prison in Berlin rather less than a year before his death. The question that disturbs him is, I believe, almost everybody's question; though its context, apart from his insistence on the inadequacy of words, well illustrates both Bonhoeffer's strength and his weakness.

> What is bothering me incessantly is the question what Christianity really is, or indeed who Christ really is, for us today. The time when people could be told everything by means of words, whether theological or pious, is over, and so is the time of inwardness and conscience—and that means the time of religion in general. We are moving towards a completely religionless time; people as they are now simply cannot be religious any more. Even those who honestly describe themselves as 'religious' do not in the least act up to it, and so they presumably mean something quite different by 'religious'.[1]

Bonhoeffer can seize with profound insight on aspects of Christianity and state them challengingly, even provocatively,

[1] Dietrich Bonhoeffer, *Letters and Papers from Prison*, SCM Press, 1971 edition, p. 279. Hereinafter referred to as *LPP*.

but he cannot work them out consistently or relate them to other equally important aspects. Given the febrile condition of Germany in the 1930s, it is understandable that an idealist of such unshakable integrity should be more eager to change the situation than to pause and analyse it carefully. Like Luther, to whose theological outlook he became more and more committed, he was a dedicated reformer. At the age of fourteen, when his brothers and sisters tried to dissuade the young Dietrich from following his vocation, on the grounds that the church to which he proposed to dedicate himself was 'a poor, feeble, boring, petty bourgeois institution', he replied confidently: 'In that case I shall reform it!' He proved faithful to his resolve and his efforts towards Church reform may still be bearing fruit.

A brief consideration of Bonhoeffer is appropriate here, in view both of the freshness of his approach and his own concern for youth. Writing at the beginning of 1943, he points out how much easier it is 'to see a thing through from the point of view of abstract principle than from that of concrete responsibility'. And he adds: 'The rising generation will always instinctively discern which of these we make the basis of our actions, for it is their own future that is at stake.' (*LPP*, p. 7.) At the age of twenty-four, in a notable tribute on the occasion of the death of Adolf von Harnack (by whom, rather than by Karl Barth, Bonhoeffer could profitably have allowed himself to be more deeply influenced) such phrases as the following occur: '. . . He made it plain to us that truth is born only of freedom. We saw in him a champion of the free expression of truth when it has been recognized . . . This made him . . . the friend of all young people who freely express their opinions, as he wanted them to do . . . we saw in him a bulwark against all trivialization and destruction, all schematization of the life of the mind.'[1]

[1] Eberhard Bethge, *Dietrich Bonhoeffer*, William Collins and Harper & Row, 1970, p. 102. Hereinafter referred to as *DB*.

'Religionless Christianity' is, I believe, at bottom an absurdity; but as there is nothing absurd about Bonhoeffer—although he was in fact charged by his critics with the position: *credo quia absurdum* (*DB*, p. 163)—the notion is worth examining. From his student days in Berlin he was reacting against the concept of the 'religious *a priori*' which dominated the thinking of one of his professors, Reinhold Seeberg (*DB*, p. 48). Bonhoeffer came to hold that an innate religious attitude, the 'religious *a priori*', did not exist at all but was a historically conditioned and transient form of human self-expression. He holds fervently to Christianity, but not to 'religion'—which he sees as not given by God as revealed in the Bible, but as devised by man in an effort to achieve his own salvation. Was the western form of Christianity perhaps only a preliminary stage to the complete absence of religion? 'How do we speak of God—without religion, i.e., without the temporally conditioned presuppositions of metaphysics, inwardness, and so on?' (*LPP*, p. 280). And the solution? 'There are degrees of knowledge and degrees of significance; that means that a secret discipline must be restored whereby the *mysteries* of the Christian faith are protected against profanation.' (*Ibid.*, p. 286.) '. . . Christ is no longer an object of religion, but something quite different, really the Lord of the world' (p. 281).

Here arises Bonhoeffer's this-worldliness. 'Aren't righteousness and the Kingdom of God on earth the focus of everything . . . ?' 'What is above this world is, in the gospel, intended to exist *for* this world; I mean that, not in the anthropocentric sense of liberal, mystic pietistic, ethical theology, but in the biblical sense of the creation and of the incarnation, crucifixion, and resurrection of Jesus Christ' (p. 286).

Understandably perhaps, Bonhoeffer was never able to work out his 'non-religious interpretation of biblical concepts;

the job is too big for me to finish just yet' (*ibid.*, p. 359). But we are led by his own characteristic logic to his best known and most fruitful formulation: 'Jesus, the man for others' (*DB*, p. 99). At first its application is confined to the bounds of the Church; later it is thought of as permanently and essentially freed from all bounds and applied to the world as belonging entirely to Christ. This, Bonhoeffer believed, embodied, or rather Christianised, the dimension of 'transcendence', removing it from the sphere of philo-sophical-metaphysical thinking and placing it within the actualities of everyday ethical and social living.

Bonhoeffer's conception of the world's 'coming of age' is difficult and not easy to make sense of. Possibly it is the most paradoxical and least meaningful element in his thought. It is important, however, as it dominated his mind during the last year of his life and seems to have been the starting point for his 'secular interpretation' of Christianity: in which enterprise he has had, and still has, many followers. Eberhard Bethge points out that in using the phrase Bonhoeffer is thinking of Kant's formula: 'The Enlightenment is the emer-gence of man from immaturity that he himself is responsible for. Immaturity is the incapacity to use one's own intelligence without the guidance of another person' (*DB*, p. 770, quoting the introductory statement of Immanuel Kant's *Was ist Aufklärung?*). This statement has embarrassed many Christian theologians, but Bonhoeffer takes Kant's descrip-tion of maturity as an essential element in the *theologia crucis*, the 'theology of the Cross'.

The phrase 'come of age' appears with variations in several contexts, but the following passage, from a letter to Eberhard Bethge dated 16 July 1944, gives us the heart of the matter:

> And we cannot be honest unless we recognize that we have to live in the world *etsi deus non daretur* (= even if God did not exist). And this is just what we do recognize—before God! God himself compels us to recognize it. So our coming of age

leads us to a true recognition of our situation before God. God would have us know that we must live as men who manage our lives without him. The God who is with us is the God who forsakes us (Mark 15.34). The God who lets us live in the world without the working hypothesis of God is the God before whom we stand continually. Before God and with God we live without God. God lets himself be pushed out of the world on to the cross. He is weak and powerless in the world, and that is precisely the way, the only way, in which he is with us and helps us. Matthew 8.17 makes it quite clear that Christ helps us, not by virtue of his omnipotence, but by virtue of his weakness and suffering.

Here is the decisive difference between Christianity and all religions. Man's religiosity makes him look in his distress to the power of God in the world: God is the *deus ex machina*. The Bible directs man to God's powerlessness and suffering; only the suffering God can help . . . (*LPP*, pp. 360–361).

This is a moving statement of a personal position, born of a sense of dereliction,[1] a *cri de coeur* forced from him by his sufferings at Tegel. As an expression of faith and devotion, based on his Lutheran presuppositions, from which he clearly derived spiritual strength, it is above criticism. But such an experience cannot be generalised into a theology, made the basis for a completely secularised Christianity, as if Christ could ever be invoked to sanction a godless world. For all his articulateness, we cannot presume to know the state of Bonhoeffer's mind towards the end of his life. The evidence of witnesses points to a wonderful serenity, a genuine holiness, indicating that he lived out his own maxim: that the true Christian should be a 'man for others'. But apart from this, what of his message?

The record shows that, as a theological student, he had first rate abilities. He sat under the acknowledged masters of his day and did not fail to impress them. Had he lived, he might well have become an outstanding theologian in the best German tradition. Yet he was a creative rather than a

[1] See my reference to Mark 15.34 on page 66.

speculative thinker; successive ideas and intuitions, not a steady vision, characterised his mind. By the time he had sent to his friends signed copies of one of his books—'his interests had again moved on elsewhere' (*DB*, p. 100). He was in many ways an extrovert, a man of action, unsatisfied by concentrated study. His biographer tells us that he was strongly motivated by an 'insatiable curiosity for every new reality' (*ibid.*, p. 122). But knowledge of himself did not much concern him: '. . . I know less than ever about myself, and I'm no longer attaching any importance to it' (*LPP*, p. 162). Hence his continuous uncertainty and self-doubt. As university lecturer, 'He still felt remote from what he wanted to understand and say, and always remained sceptical about the answers he had established' (*DB*, p. 161). Later we find him writing to Karl Barth: 'I feel that in some way I don't understand I have somehow got up against all my friends . . . All this has frightened me and shaken my confidence so that I begin to fear that dogmatism might be leading me astray . . .' (*ibid.*, p. 254).

In some respects these admissions make him all the more impressive: they show his Christian awareness that theology is less important than right action, the engaging modesty which allows that he may be wrong. What does affect his message, however, is his incapacity for abstract thought; his inability to evaluate traditional Christian ideas on their merits. The remedy for these shortcomings, had he been able to receive it, he could have acquired from Harnack, whom, as a young student, he contradicts politely and later criticises to his fellow students. The complaint? That he lingers over the *Epistle of St Clement* instead of moving on to the Reformation. Throughout his life, Bonhoeffer is disputatious rather than constructively critical; he moves from position to position on the circumference, unanchored in any central viewpoint. His philosophy, such as it is, is nominalist, like that of his great hero, Luther, whom, though he admits

would probably have held very different opinions today, he
never really criticises—in the way, for example, that Kierkegaard does: Luther 'did inestimable harm by the fact that he
did not become a martyr'; 'he was a confused pate, who
lifted burdens off' . . . and hence was 'the very opposite of an
apostle'. 'He took man's part against God.'

Bonhoeffer follows Kierkegaard in his either/or rather
than both/and attitude to almost every situation, but the
latter had much the more powerful intelligence. All his life
he was confessedly influenced by the Platonic Socrates,
Bonhoeffer not at all. He read a book called *The Gods of
Greece* and found these gods 'less offensive than certain brands
of Christianity' (*LPP*, p. 333), yet the Greek philosophers,
Plato and Aristotle, are apparently unopened books for him.
Understandably so, for Bonhoeffer was inveterately anti-
speculative and anti-mystical; he wished 'to accept the concrete world as much as possible'. His dialectical thinking was
not polarised between the seen and the unseen, appearance
and reality; it was focused on what he believed to be the
biblical, eschatological tension between 'no longer' and 'not
yet' (*DB*, p. 61). He criticises the doctrine—clearly stated in
Augustine and the great mediaeval theologians (whom he
never studied)—of the immanence of the Trinity within the
human spirit, and yet he can say: 'God is nearer to me than
my existence is, in as much as it is he who first discloses my
existence to me' (*ibid.*, p. 99).

Bonhoeffer criticises religion from the standpoint of
Christology. He does not notice that, though the New
Testament is Christocentric, Jesus himself is theocentric.
Jesus was the man for, or with, God, before he was the 'man
for others'. In his *The Cost of Discipleship*, studded with New
Testament references, Bonhoeffer has very little to say
of the Logos doctrine of St John. Amid the fourteen references to the Epistle to the Hebrews, 13.8 significantly
does not appear: 'Jesus Christ the same yesterday and today

and for ever.' This text points to a transcendence other than, though not necessarily incompatible with, 'the neighbour who is within reach in any given situation'. 'The transcendence of epistemological theory', writes Bonhoeffer, 'has nothing to do with the transcendence of God' (*LPP*, p. 282). But dogmatism of this kind will hardly do, if faith is to seek understanding and the work of Augustine, Anselm and Aquinas is not to go for nothing.

Christianity is both worldly and unworldly, in time and beyond time. Despite himself, Bonhoeffer must have been aware that this was so; and for all his protests against the 'religious *a priori*', he could not escape from it. St Augustine's *Confessions* are addressed to God, not to Christ: the well known words in the opening chapter: 'You have made us for yourself, and our heart is restless until it rests in you'—are the classical statement of the inateness of the religious impulse. Eberhard Bethge tells us that while a pastor in Barcelona, Bonhoeffer quoted these words 'in his first and last sermons and several in between'. Though later he may have withdrawn from a position so clearly tinged with Platonic philosophy, it was only to fall into what may fairly be described as a biblical-Lutheran *a priori* of his own.

If Bonhoeffer's writings unintentionally prepared the way for a perhaps too unqualified secularisation of religion, and even the absurdity of a 'Christianity without God', nothing can detract from the integrity of his personal witness. He was aware of his own deficiencies (he wished for dialogue and criticism) and the limitations of his environment. Reflecting on the theological scene after his visit to America, he writes: 'Looked at from across the Atlantic, our standpoint and our theology look so local, and it seems inconceivable that in the whole of the world just Germany, and in Germany just a few men, have understood what the Gospel is. And yet I see a message nowhere else.' (*DB*, p. 122.) His biographer points out that Bonhoeffer's spiritual ardour concealed a certain scepticism combined with a thirst for knowledge. From London he writes: '. . . since I am becoming daily more convinced that in the West Christianity is approaching its end—at least in its present form, and its present interpretation—I should like to go to the Far East before coming back to Germany' (*DB*, pp. 329–330). Perhaps the real tragedy of his life was the non-fulfilment of his desire to do just that. Had he done so, how different his life work might have turned out to be!

When he was twenty-two, his maternal grandmother had written to him: 'In your place I should try some time or other to get to know the contrasting world of the East. I am thinking of India, Buddha and his world' (*ibid.*, p. 74). This bold suggestion left its mark and later, in one of his letters to her, we find him referring to the story of Buddha, from which he derived some inspiration. Had he met with Gandhi, as plans had been worked out for him to do, his resistance to Hitler's regime might have taken a different course. Not surprisingly, even the discerning among the clerical circle of his friends in Berlin failed to understand his secret hankering after India and his interest in Gandhi's method of resistance. What might have resulted had he been able to do what he so greatly wanted—'to be brought face to face with Indian answers to the problem of living as a counter-point to his own philosophy and theology' (*ibid.*, p. 107), we can only guess.

He would doubtless have reacted unfavourably to aspects of Indian life, and with his eye for the concrete situation, have looked dubiously on certain manifestations of Hinduism. But with his keen intelligence and desire for knowledge, he would quickly have moved behind the scenes. What would he have made of a Brahmin expounding the *tat tvam asi* doctrine of the Upanishads, or of a presentation of Nagarjuna's Buddhist philosophy? Less than nothing—had he been unable to break free from his anti-speculative, anti-metaphysical, anti-mystical, anti-'inwardness' prejudices. On the other hand, his mind might have undergone its own 'Copernican revolution', and he could have returned to Europe to discover that significant religious thinking did not after all begin with the Reformation. He could have turned to the work of Rudolph Otto (a contemporary German theologian of immense reputation whom Bonhoeffer seems deliberately to have ignored) and pondered such a passage as the following:

> *Jnana* (i.e., intuitive knowledge of the ground of being) is eternal, is general, is necessary and is not a personal know-ledge of this man or that man. It is there, as knowledge in the *Atman* (i.e., the Self) itself, and lies there hidden under all *avidya* (i.e., ignorance)—irremovable, though it may be obscured, unprovable, because self-evident, needing no proof, because itself giving to all proof the ground of possi-bility. These sentences come near to Eckhart's 'knowledge' and to the teaching of Augustine on the Eternal Truth in the soul which, itself immediately certain, is the ground of all certainty and is a possession, not of A or B, but of 'the soul'.[1]

There he could have learned that a religious tradition, parallel to that of India, was already alive in mediaeval Catholicism. Like Mahayana Buddhism, it insisted that salva-tion is a pure gift not at man's command; it provided safe-guards against the *hubris* (which Bonhoeffer rightly regarded as the supreme sin) as effectively as anything in Luther's distinctive message. From the Mahayana he could also have learned that the 'man for others' was its central theme, em-bodied in the Bodhisattva ideal, which has been formulated succinctly in practical terms by Shantideva: 'Whoever wishes quickly to rescue himself and another, should practise the supreme mystery: the exchanging of himself and the other.'

Bonhoeffer's limitations were no more than the defects of his qualities. Honest and courageous to a degree which it is presumptuous to praise, he insisted that Christianity must

[1] Quoted from Aldous Huxley, *The Perennial Philosophy*, Harper & Row, New York and London, 1944, 1945, p. 131.

prove itself in action. When the impulse stirred him he could focus his thought with unerring clarity, as for instance in this observation on chastity: 'The essence of chastity is not the suppresion of lust, but the total orientation of one's life towards a goal. Without such a goal, chastity is bound to become ridiculous. Chastity is the *sine qua non* of lucidity and concentration' (*LPP*, p. 376). Though the field was un-explored by him, he had what might be called the 'Zen Catholic' insight: 'The beyond is not what is infinitely remote, but what is nearest at hand' (*ibid.*). Deeply prayer-ful and in sympathy with the contemplative life, he would make visits to the Benedictine monastery at Ettal. His distaste for vagueness in religion ensured that he would never lose the concept of 'the Church' once it had been acquired, chiefly by his experiences in Rome. Bethge writes: 'The fascination exercised by Catholic Rome became a permanent influence on Bonhoeffer's thought' (*DB*, p. 38). 'Devotion to the "Church" such as he met here, the sense of uni-versalism of the ecclesia, was something new to him.' 'I went for a short walk on the Pincio', he wrote in his diary. 'It had been a magnificent day; the first on which I gained some real understanding of Catholicism; no romanticism or any-thing of that sort, but I believe I am beginning to under-stand the concept of the Church.'

Bonhoeffer's spirit lives on. He has earned the right to give counsel to the Church and to be listened to. In an outline for an unwritten book, he captured the ethos of living Christi-anity, set the tone for perhaps the only kind of churchman-ship that can inspire the younger generation of today. 'The church is the church only when it exists for others.'

> The church must share in the secular problems of ordinary human life, not dominating, but helping and serving. It must tell men of every calling what it means to live in Christ, to exist for others. In particular, our own church will have to take the field against the vices of *hubris*, power-worship, envy

and humbug, as the roots of all evil. It will have to speak
of moderation, purity, trust, loyalty, constancy, patience,
discipline, humility, contentment, and modesty. It must not
under-estimate the importance of human example (which
has its origin in the humanity of Jesus and is so important in
Paul's teaching); it is not abstract argument, but example,
that gives its word emphasis and power. (*LPP*, pp. 382–383.)

Yet something more than speech and example is required
if, spiritually speaking, we are to renew our youth. An
experience of awakening, a sense that, whatever our age, we
are still children of God, needs to be prayed for, with the
mind still and receptive, the heart compassionately open.
Christian simplicity demands, as Aldous Huxley observed,
that 'one must get rid of all the rigidities of unregenerate
adulthood and become again as a little child'. Old age tends
to cling to its meagre joys and lament the sorrow, forgetful
that happiness is always counterpointed by sadness. To be
young in spirit, however physically old one may be, is to act
out spontaneously the deep wisdom of Blake's lines:

> He who binds to himself a joy
> Does the wingèd life destroy,
> But he who kisses the joy as it flies
> Lives in eternity's surprise.

7   Arranging what we have always known

Recapitulation

WE HAVE seen outlined in the preceding chapters: how Christianity as a religion of salvation, at first regarded as a compelling summons of great urgency, came to be established within the political and social structure of the Roman empire; to be articulated by rational philosophy; to be challenged as it existed under the Papacy as a betrayal of its origins, and beneath the cumulative weight of scientific knowledge, biblical criticism and man's global consciousness, to be seen, at least in its present form, as providing but one among many answers to the problems of human existence. We were led to inquire into the nature of the salvation offered by the Church, to note that it had to do with the attainment of truth and freedom, but also that attention was focused more and more upon doctrinal statements propounded by ecclesiastical authority. The assurance that the Church could proclaim its dogmas infallibly made a strong appeal to minds searching for security, even though it did not necessarily bring them to the unitive knowledge of the One, 'whose service is perfect freedom'.

We next discussed some of the lessons that might be learned from the religions of the East, specifically the Hindu-Buddhist tradition. Here was a challenge to routine Christianity to enter its own depths and to broaden its understanding of the Incarnation—investigations sanctioned by the Second

Vatican Council. Some lessons we might learn from Buddhist meditation and its underlying philosophy were touched on, with special reference to living in the present and attaining inner freedom. Following this, a new look was taken at Christianity, as we re-examined briefly the implications of participating in the divine nature and being children of God. The next step was to comment in general terms on the state of today's younger generation. Here seemed the natural place to attempt to evaluate the contribution of a relatively young theologian, Dietrich Bonhoeffer, who died tragically in 1945, but whose influence on Christian thought endures. It only remains for us to bring these various though related considerations into a single focus.

Finding the context

Within what frame of reference are we now to consider the content oᶠ the Christian faith? Faith itself, according to St Thomas Aquinas, is a 'beatifying knowledge'. Here is his summary of its content: 'The Lord taught that this beatifying knowledge bears upon two known realities, namely the divineness of the Trinity and the humanity of Christ: who accordingly spoke thus to the Father: "And this is eternal life, that they know thee the only true God, and Jesus Christ whom thou hast sent" (John 17.3). Therefore the entire knowledge of faith turns on these two: namely the divineness of the Trinity and the humanity of Christ.'[1] The Church can still authenticate herself as the guardian of the Christian tradition by an appeal to an ancient formula: 'The word of the Lord that has come down to us either orally or in the scriptures.' But today it is hardly enough to cite the official creeds or examine the Bible in the light of those creeds. We

[1] 'Illam autem beatificantem cognitionem circa duo cognita Dominus consistere docuit: scilicet circa Divinitatem Trinitatis, et humanitatem Christi: unde ad Patrem loquens, dicit (Joan. 17,3): "Haec est vita aeterna, ut cognoscant te Deum verum, et quem misisti Jesum Christum." Circa haec ergo duo tota fidei cognitio versatur: scilicet circa Divinitatem Trinitatis, et humanitatem Christi.' St Thomas Aquinas, *Compendium Theologiae*, cap. 2.

now know, as certainly as such matters can be known, that the four gospels draw upon earlier sources. They present Jesus as faithfully as their several authors knew how, but with a variety of listeners and readers, as well as an underlying theological purpose in mind. The evangelists were concerned not merely to tell it as it was, as far as they were able to do so, but also to meet the inquiries, needs and aspirations, of the believing communities among which the gospels circulated.

Then St Paul appears upon the scene. With him emerges the question, arising from our earliest sources and still not satisfactorily answered: what is Christianity? The headquarters of the primitive Church were at Jerusalem—and so they remained until that city was destroyed by the Romans in the year AD 70. Included in the destruction was the disappearance of whatever written records existed of the Jerusalem Church; but that it did not accept at his own valuation the message of Paul can be gathered from the New Testament evidence. The early Jerusalem community regarded Jesus, whom they had personally known, as a crucified prophet. They believed that he had risen from the dead, thereby establishing his Messiahship, and that he would shortly appear again as the Son of Man to bring into being for ever the Kingdom of God.

St Paul went further than this: he attached to the crucifixion a saving value that extended to gentiles as well as Jews. His vision was of the resurrected Christ who made possible a new mode of existence for all men. Paul would have had everyone enjoy his own ecstatic experience of the risen Jesus. In his attempts to bring this about he preached a message in a way that would be acceptable not only to Jews—it was unwelcome, even repugnant, to many of them—but to those already influenced by the current religious philosophies of the Graeco-Roman world. To Paul more than to any other individual of whom we have record, apart from its Founder, belongs the credit of transforming Christianity from a Jewish sect into the religion of the western world.

But now, as we have seen acknowledged by Vatican II, the cultural background has widened still further. India and the Far East are no longer to be regarded merely as a field for Christian missionary endeavour. Monologue has given place to dialogue: the spiritual and moral values cherished by adherents of the Hindu-Buddhist tradition are to be respected in their own right. A religious structure that was largely built up to sanction the unity and continuity of the Roman empire could hardly compass the metaphysics of the Vedanta or the fluidity of Mahayana Buddhism. In these areas a somewhat legalistic theology, appropriate to classical Christendom, has been found inapplicable. All of which raises a profound question which will only be presented here. Its full discussion must be left to theologians wiser and more learned than the present writer, its final solution to those who can speak with authority.

Referring to 'Jesus Christ of Nazareth', the account in Acts of the Apostles continues: 'And there is salvation in no one else, for there is no other name under heaven given among men by which we must be saved' (Acts 4.12). Elsewhere we find: 'For there is one God, and there is one mediator between God and men, the man Christ Jesus, who gave himself as a ransom for all . . .' (1 Timothy 2.5). Let the truth of these well known scriptural texts, and others like them, remain unchallenged. They are still to be understood against the mental background of the inspired writers who composed them, and in accordance with the character of the Church tradition by which they were proclaimed. No positive verbal statement can be absolutised; it must be related to the speaker, the hearer, and the situation in which it is spoken. We touch here, of course, on the central doctrine of the Incarnation—the content of which is implicit in the present essay. But does Christianity's preemptive claim with respect to the world's salvation, by virtue of the one 'name' and the only 'mediator', definitively rule out parallel doctrines familiar in the East from before the Christian era? It is a commonplace of Hinduism that the Godhead is manifested in everyone: salvation or liberation, consists in *realising* that this is so. And here is the ultimate position of Mahayana Buddhism, as presented by an authoritative exponent. Referring to the Buddha as the Absolute, Professor Murti writes: 'As possessed of Karuna (= active compassion) and owing to his essential equality with all beings, he is in the region of phenomena. He is thus an amphibious being, having one foot in the Absolute and the other in phenomena. And it is because of this that he performs the function of mediator between the two.'[1]

If these positions were acknowledged by Christians, would anything be lost other than a sense of exclusiveness? Not 'the divineness of the Trinity or the humanity of Christ', not the doctrine of the Logos, not the wonder and inspiration of the life, death and resurrection of Jesus, not anything of the Church as the mystical body of Christ, not even the singular position of authority belonging to St Peter (Matthew 16.18), which is a part of the earliest tradition. And what a flood of light these widening perspectives might throw upon the personality of Jesus himself! In this context the present climate of opinion in the Church may be more receptive than it was forty years ago of the view cogently expressed by B. H. Streeter in his *The Buddha and The Christ* (Macmillan, 1932, p. 216): 'Theologians have commonly imagined that they are under obligation to make a complete isolation of the sacrifice of Christ from the heroic self-offering of other noble souls; and this has vitiated most of the classical attempts to produce a doctrine of the Atonement. Just so a similar isolation of the divine sonship of Christ from the potentiality

[1] T. R. V. Murti, *The Central Philosophy of Buddhism*, George Allen and Unwin, 1955, p. 284.

in other men "to become the sons of God" (John 1.12) has defeated the attempt to produce a satisfactory doctrine of the Incarnation.' Whatever conclusion this line of thought may eventually lead to, let us rest content for the moment with the proposition that Christianity is Christ, and proceed to review some of the difficulties in the way of realising this ideal.

The Church's difficulties

Much of what has recently been written about the Church takes the form of a literature of protest. This is understandable but in some ways a pity. Eagerness to change the ecclesiastical structure has outstripped, and in many cases replaced the effort required to comprehend why things are the way they are. Once more, perhaps, such matters are viewed more patiently in the East than in the West. There is a law of karma which applies to institutions no less than to individuals. Action or deliberate inaction brings in its train a series of consequences, good or bad, which nothing can stop, nothing can alter. Release from this karmic sequence is possible for the individual—this is precisely what is meant by spiritual liberation—but not for an institution such as the Church, in so far as it is bound up with the warp and woof of human history. Faithful to the original message of Christ, responding to the promptings of his Spirit, the Church today is the product of nearly two millennia of good karma. But intermingled with this is the bad karma set in motion by the infidelities in high places: the concern for personal power and prestige, the compromises with political interests, the refusals to face inconvenient truth, the persecutions, the unworthy popes and bishops, the inquisition, the excessive legalism, the defensiveness born of fear and anger—all this and much else has brought about the condition of the Church as she now exists. It is the inevitable harvest, the weeds along with the wheat, of the seed which for over nineteen centuries she has sown. Those at present in positions of authority are not responsible for this state of affairs; they have inherited it; when truly representing the Church, they deserve our sympathy and support. The only valid criticism is that which might contribute to bringing the Church corporately to a higher state of enlightenment—and here the obvious place to begin is with one's own self-criticism.

It is sometimes forgotten that, were it not for the Church, the world would know nothing of Christ. However inadequate institutional Christianity may appear, its constructive contribution to human welfare should not be minimised. The Church is in fact an extension of the Incarnation which she presents to the world of every day. By the world of every day we mean the vast majority of the faithful who have neither the time nor inclination to ponder religious problems, but who look to Church authority to provide them with a doctrinal and moral framework within which they can lead acceptable Christian lives. These millions of ordinary people are churchmen's first responsibility in what they teach and ordain; quite secondary are the spiritual requirements of scholars, philosophers, or even mystics. Thus the Church on any showing offers its members, individually and collectively, a means of communication with something higher and more significant than self; she proposes a way of life that encourages both self-giving and self-restraint, and provides a form of worship expressive of love as well as faith, together with an assured link with Christianity's historic origins.

At the same time, both givers and receivers in this process need to become increasingly aware of the limitations of what is offered—or rather of the manner, perhaps the only manner, in which it can be offered. As we have noted earlier, the Church as an institution operates externally, with signs in the form of verbal teaching and symbols in the form of sacraments. What happens to these signs and symbols at the receiving end lies outside the church's jurisdiction; it depends on the vitality of the recipient's faith, considered as conscious awareness. By some they are accepted with a kind of fundamentalist literalism, by others as indications of something numinous lying beyond the senses, by others as occasions for petitionary prayer or selfless devotion, by others almost routinely as medicine for personal shortcomings. In sum, the effectiveness of the Church's routine ministrations, for all the grace-imparting quality of the sacraments, is conditioned by the state of mind of those who receive them. An individual's spiritual life may be fostered by outside influences, as a plant flourishes beneath sunshine and rain, but the growth to maturity comes from the inner depths, from the root which is the spirit itself. The institutional aspects of the Church and the externals of the liturgy, including the sacraments, are parts of the phenomenal world—just as Christ's humanity was, hiding his divinity. We are meant to pass beyond them. Thus Christians can make their own the often quoted prayer from the Brihadaranyaka Upanishad:

> From the unreal lead me to the real,
> from darkness lead me to light,
> from the mortal lead me to the immortal.

Uniting the inward and the outward

The distinguished theologian Emil Brunner once observed: 'The transfer of faith from the dimension of personal encounter into the dimension of factual instruction is the great tragedy in the history of Christianity.' Clearly this is a challenging statement, in line with much that is implied in these pages. It emphasises the point that indoctrination can at best supply religion only at second hand. None the less it overlooks the fact, which we have also stressed, that a personal encounter with God as manifested in Christ is possible now, without any appeal to the past. The quest for the historical Jesus may be enthralling, but it is not one on whose outcome the faith of a Christian depends. Not all those who encountered Jesus face to face became believers. What made the difference was the presence of Jesus' Spirit after his resurrection. 'No one can say "Jesus is Lord" except by the Holy Spirit' (1 Corinthians 12.3). And further: '. . . he who is united to the Lord becomes one spirit with him' (6.17). The abiding sequel to this situation is not a state of emotional euphoria—the excitement of being able to 'speak with tongues', for example—but the ability to follow St Paul's 'still more excellent way'. 'If I speak in the tongues of men and of angels, but have not love, I am a noisy gong or a clanging cymbal . . .' (13.1ff.).

These texts are not quoted in any spirit of biblical funda-mentalism—which would be to sponsor a retrograde Christianity—but because they represent a permanent factor in religion. Paradoxically the need today, I suggest, is not to focus on what is distinctively Christian: salvation history, theories of redemption, a theology of hope—but to show how Christianity manifests through history, as emerging in space and time, a religion that is eternal. Bringing together what appears externally and what lies hidden in the life of the human spirit, will involve us more in a consideration of the religion *of* Jesus than of religion *about* Jesus—that factual instruction which has hitherto been the chief concern of orthodox Christianity.

In the biblical language familiar to his hearers, Jesus pointed to the essentials of the religion which he shared with them: they were to love God with all their heart, soul, mind and strength (Mark 12.30); that is to say, in modern terminology, they were to identify totally with God, and similarly, through God-dedication, with their neighbour (v. 31). Taken separately these requirements are to be found in pre-Christian Judaism (Deuteronomy 6.4; Leviticus 19.18); though Jesus may have been the first to link them explicitly together. At any rate they bring us to the roots of all the higher religions. From these roots have sprung flowers whose method of cultivation may be different but whose nature is the same. Four fundamental doctrines, neatly summarised by Aldous Huxley,[1] underlie the religions of the East:

> First: the phenomenal world of matter and of individualized consciousness—the world of things and animals and men and even gods—is the manifestation of a Divine Ground within which all partial realities have their being, and apart from which they would be non-existent.
>
> Second: human beings are capable not merely of knowing *about* the Divine Ground by inference; they can also realise its existence by a direct intuition, superior to discursive reasoning. This immediate knowledge unites the knower with that which is known.
>
> Third: man possesses a double nature, a phenomenal ego and an eternal self, which is the inner man, the spirit, the spark of divinity within the soul. It is possible for man, if he so desires, to identify himself with the spirit and therefore with the Divine Ground, which is of the same or like nature with the spirit.
>
> Fourth: man's life on earth has only one end and purpose: to identify himself with the eternal self and so come to the knowledge of the Divine Ground.

As has already emerged, hints of these very doctrines can be discovered, at least in embryo, in the earliest Christian writings as their authors sought acceptance in the Hellenistic world. First: we find St Paul making the point to the community of believers at Corinth: 'we look not to the things that are seen but to the things that are unseen; for the things that are seen are transient, but the things that are unseen are eternal' (2 Corinthians 4.18). Moreover he is reported to have urged the Athenians to seek after the God in whom 'we live and move and have our being' (Acts 17.27–28). Second: not only Jesus, conceived as God's incarnate Word, must be known, but God himself—'And this is eternal life, that they

[1] Introduction to the *Bhagavad-Gita*. Translated by Swami Prabhavananda and Christopher Isherwood. A Mentor Book. The New American Library. Copyright 1944, 1951 by the Vedanta Society of Southern California.

know thee the only true God . . .' (John 17.3). Third: man's double nature could hardly be more emphatically affirmed than it is by St Paul: 'For I delight in the law of God, in my inmost self, but I see in my members another law at war with the law of my mind . . .' (Romans 7.22–23). Yet he finds it a matter of experience that God's Spirit testifies to our spirit that we are his children (8.16). A similar message is conveyed in a later New Testament document, the import of which has already been discussed—that we may 'escape from the corruption that is in the world because of passion, and become partakers of the divine nature' (2 Peter 1.4). Fourth: finally, the great eschatological climax—that God may be all in all, 'everything to every one' (1 Corinthians 15.28).

This having been said, Christians will rightly look upon Jesus as the model of the religious person. He exemplified what he taught about the primacy of love, showing that love for God and love of neighbour cannot really be separated. How we treat, positively or negatively, those we come into contact with is the test of our attitude to God. The people near at hand and available, as Bonhoeffer wrote, are the 'transcendent'. Nevertheless, Jesus' love for mankind, and ours in so far as we reflect it, cannot be reduced to humanitarian kindliness. A Christian's active compassion should result from knowledge, a profound insight comparable to that of Christ. His life of self-giving was made possible by his knowledge of the Father and the assurance that this gave him. St John records a tradition, in part at least, from which we can gather that Jesus' closest disciples may actually have heard these words: 'O righteous Father, the world has not known thee, but I have known thee; and these know that thou hast sent me. I made known to them thy name, and I will make it known, that the love with which thou hast loved me may be in them, and I in them' (John 17.25–26). This is the unitive knowledge in which to some degree we may share, as St Paul claimed to do: '. . . we have the mind of Christ' (1 Corinthians 2.16).

Love for God is not an active taking possession but a response based on knowledge. In the Lord's Prayer there is no mention of the singular 'I', only of 'Thou' and the communal 'we'. The petitions seek for an ever increasing harmony—'Thy kingdom come, Thy will be done'. . . . 'Forgive us as we forgive.' As God's kingdom comes and his will is done, and we are reconciled one with another, the ignorance caused by, and which causes, sin diminishes and we become more consciously what we are. That by which we exist, the Godhead, the Divine Ground, *realises* itself and we are no longer at odds with ourselves or with other people. To the Christian understanding, this flooding of the human consciousness with a share in God's knowledge and love takes place in and with the risen Lord. 'It is no longer I who live, but Christ who lives in me' (Galatians 2.20).

To paraphrase the thought of Paul Tillich: Jesus as the particular manifestation of the Divine became the Christ, the 'new being'. The new being is the power beyond man's natural consciousness that heals his existential conflicts and overcomes his sin—sin being understood as his estrangement from himself, from others and from the ground of his being. 'Putting on Christ'—to use the Pauline phrase (Galatians 3.27)—means that we ourselves share in the new being which Christ is. None of this takes place in isolation. The French Catholic existentialist, Gabriel Marcel, sees a chain of four notions, successive but overlapping, which indicate the movement towards realisation. They are: person—engagement—community—reality. In other words, only by engaging ourselves in community can we reach reality. The Godhead must be recognised within the depths of the spirit, and also in the people around us and in the world of nature. Not to find God everywhere is not to find him truly anywhere.

The importance of uniting appropriately outward conduct with the inner spirit, so that the one is the expression of the other, cannot be exaggerated. Bordering the path to liberation and enlightenment, as untutored seekers have sometimes found, there are 'cliffs of fall frightful'. Illuminism, as an unauthenticated inner light, and antinomianism, as radical lawlessness, are the penalties often paid when mystical experience is looked upon as the only criterion for genuine religion. By their fruits you shall know them. A notable list of these fruits, which cannot be recalled too often, is supplied by St Paul, who boasted of having Christ's own enlightenment and had no time for any externally imposed law: 'But the fruit of the Spirit is love, joy, peace, patience, kindness, goodness, faithfulness, self-control; against such there is no law' (Galatians 5.22).

No external law, that is—because 'he who does what is true comes to the light' (John 3.21); his would-be autonomy has given place to theonomy: the law by which he lives is not separate from Reality itself. Thus the New Testament recalls the prophecy of Jeremiah (31.31–34):

> This is the covenant I will make with the house of Israel
> after those days, says the Lord:
> I will put my laws into their minds,
> and write them on their hearts,
> and I will be their God,
> and they shall be my people.
> And they shall not teach every one his fellow
> or every one his brother, saying,
> 'Know the Lord,'
> for all shall know me,
> from the least of them to the greatest (Hebrews 8.10–11).

Over the centuries the Church has worked out a fairly specific ethical code, but none of its requirements can be turned into moral absolutes. Circumstances alter cases and here, if anywhere, it is the letter that kills while the spirit gives life (cf. 2 Corinthians 3.6). A general principle of conduct is laid down by the Lord himself: 'Whatever you wish that men would do to you, do so to them' (Matthew 7.12). This was once criticised irreverently by Bernard Shaw, on the grounds that tastes differ and that we should not project on to other people our own likes and dislikes. What he did not notice is that in such a broad rule-of-thumb the positive includes the negative: we should not do to others what we would not have them do to us. Probably more mistakes are made by action than inaction, by what we do rather than by what we omit. For instance, a line of conduct based on the principle of never saying or doing anything that harms anyone, including ourselves, will save us from labouring too scrupulously over the specifics of morality. In this context the Hindu-Buddhist tradition speaks of *ahimsa*, which means 'not hurting'—an area which Christianity has by no means fully explored. But if we want the Christian way of life to be presented in more positive terms, then we must turn to the topic of worship.

From worship to communion

There can be few greater fallacies than to confuse the concept of worship with that of a church service. Worship derives from the word 'worth' and means to give to an object its due worth. Supreme worship can of course be given only to God—but to God immanent as well as transcendent, to God as manifested throughout his creation, and yet whom 'the highest heaven cannot contain' (1 Kings 8.27). Worship of the God who is 'in heaven' will involve us in the kind of devotional activities performed in church, publicly with a congregation or in small groups or just by ourselves. On the other hand, the worshipper 'in spirit and truth', for whom God is an ever-present reality, will have a sense of reverence for people and for the world of nature, since God is manifesting himself in them. Thus to abuse or mindlessly exploit the resources of nature can be regarded as a form of profanation of the divine. From which it follows that efforts to prevent heedless damage to human environment reach out to matters of much more than merely secular concern.

But let us now confine ourselves to worship as this is conventionally understood. Much has been said in the preceding pages about the necessity of interiorising religion, by way of counterbalancing a lip service which is often, unfortunately, no more than that. It must be kept in mind, however, that, as in our relations with one another so in those with God, 'they do not love who do not show their love'. External forms of worship—visible sacrifice, prostrations, song and dance—are as much, perhaps more, a part of the Hindu-Buddhist tradition as they are of Christianity. An abstract theologian like Shankara, the great exponent of the Vedanta, composed hymns of an almost erotic quality. St Thomas Aquinas and Eckhart in the West, minds of a similar metaphysical bent, would at times express their devotion to God as transcendent with the simplicity of children.

Among the most satisfactory forms of personal worship is to utter some sacred aspiration aloud, or quietly to oneself, just as a devout Hindu or Buddhist will focus his mind with a form of prayer called *mantra*. The fourteenth-century masterpiece of spiritual instruction *The Cloud of Unknowing* recommends the repetition of single words—'God' or 'Jesus' or even 'Love'—as a means of bringing the mind to rest at a single point. It is surely a matter for curiosity that the official Church must still depend for her prayer-life on pre-Christian documents, the Psalms. Meanwhile, redolent of the New Testament, there remain the never-too-familiar Our Father and Hail Mary. Here is admirable material for Christian mantras, which could effectively parallel the famous *Om Mani Padme Hum* which many young Westerners have learned from Tibet. For instance: 'Thy kingdom come, Thy will be done'—what more suitable formula for self-transcendence could conceivably be devised? Or, 'Hail Mary, full of grace, the Lord is with thee'—the perfect salutation to divinised femininity! The thought occurs, in passing, that if the right person set these to music and taught youngsters to chant them prayerfully over and over again, he might be making a contribution to their and the Church's well-being greater than he could dream of.

Worship in spirit and truth leads to union, or rather communion, with that which is worshipped. We can even remind ourselves of a verse from the Upanishads: 'Whoever worships a deity, thinking he is another and I am another, is in ignorance.' Worship which falls short of communion, with God and one's fellow-worshippers, is to some extent a turning to God without really turning away from one's egoistic self. On this topic William Law (1686–1761) had some memorable things to say:

> Would you know whence it is that so many false spirits have appeared in the world, who having deceived themselves and others with false fire and false light, laying claim to information, illumination and openings of the divine life, particularly to do wonders under extraordinary calls from God? It is this: they have turned to God without turning from themselves; would be alive to God before they are dead to their own nature. Now religion in the hands of self, or corrupt nature, serves only to discover vices of a worse kind than in nature left to itself. Hence are all the disorderly passions of religious men, which burn in a worse flame than passions only employed about worldly matters; pride, self-exaltation, hatred and persecution, under a cloak of religious zeal, will sanctify actions which nature, left to itself, would be ashamed to own.

' "Turning to God without turning from self"—the formula is absurdly simple; and yet, simple as it is, it explains all the follies and iniquities committed in the name of religion.'[1]

[1] The whole passage quoted from Aldous Huxley, *The Perennial Philosophy*, Harper & Brothers, 1945, p. 243.

Communion takes place existentially through inter-personal relationships; it is achieved symbolically by means of liturgy and sacraments. Liturgy and sacraments are means to the unitive knowledge of God—of which love, as active compassion, is the necessary complement—not ends in them-selves. Just as the institutional Church needs to be seen through, as transparent to the mystical Body of Christ, rather than challenged, so her sacramental system must be recognised as operating only—though, given the requisite predispositions, most effectively—at the level of signs and symbols. They are not themselves the essence of religion in spirit and truth. This being said, we may conclude these considerations with some remarks on the supreme sacrament, round which the Church's daily life centres, the Eucharist. The word connotes thanksgiving, so that the appropriate mood among those taking part should be one of gratitude—to God, just for his happy-making existence, for giving us our existence, and for the existence of the whole world and of the people around us.

The eucharistic materials of food and drink, bread and wine, make it a worldly as well as a heavenly communal feast. Whatever a detached onlooker might think, no one can be in any doubt about the life-enhancing power of a realistically conducted eucharistic celebration. At the worldly level, now very much being emphasized, a eucharist can be almost 'religionless' (in Bonhoeffer's sense): down-to-earth, un-stylized, without ecclesiastical trappings: a reminder that the material things God made, the whole world itself and all humanity in it, are good and therefore to be loved. The strongly felt wish, especially with the young, to have Mass, not in a large church, but like Christ's farewell supper, in a 'room' (Mark 14.15) typifies the trend to domesticate the Christian religion. A de-professionalised clergy could more easily give the lead: presiding as first among equals amid those signifying communion with one another by sharing the

consecrated bread and wine. In such a setting the Mass is
not so much a service which people 'attend', as a love-feast
in which they take part. In this and in other ways, serving
the world that God so loved, by personal integrity and an
active concern for social justice, the Church's representatives
would reveal her true nature, even while the ecclesiastical
structure may be dissolving. A loving solidarity within the
participating group—that is what wide-awake young people
hope to find nowadays at a celebration of the Eucharist.
Church authority acts wisely in not seeking to circumscribe
these hopes, however odd the attempts at their fulfilment
may sometimes seem.

On the other hand the Eucharist's dimension of transcendence must never be lost sight of. Stately ceremonial, a
century's old ritual in an ancient language, Gregorian chant,
intervening periods of complete silence—all were reminders
that the Mass, though very much of the here and now,
transported us also to another world. That these should have
been so swiftly swept away indicates a failure on the Church's
part to appreciate her own treasures. The conservative
instinct in today's world is not strong enough to warrant
widespread liturgical uniformity, but the sensibilities of
people wedded to long established custom are clearly to be
respected. Therefore those two bugbears of the authoritarian
mind, freedom and diversity, are not only to be tolerated but
welcomed—a traditional Latin Mass here, an informal yet
reverential vernacular Eucharist there. And a compromise
between the two? Perhaps—even though the least satisfactory of all: until time allows those who deal with these
matters to evolve liturgical forms that offend neither the
reason nor the ear, and an appropriate selection of scripture
readings that can be listened to without bewilderment.

The fellowship with one another which the Eucharist
symbolises is in and with Christ. It is an outward sign of the
Incarnation itself; its purpose is to stimulate the Christ-life

already latent within all who take part in the act of communion. Church tradition teaches that, unlike earthly food
which we assimilate and transform into our own bodies, this
spiritual food transforms us into itself—its underlying *reality*
(*res sacramenti*) being the union of the mystical Body of Christ.
Turning to God, and at the same time turning away from
our separative self, we are freed for union with the truest
Self, the only real '*I am*' (cf. John 4.26; 8.23, 28, 58; 14.6).
This union can be thought of as a reaching both vertically
upwards to the heights (or downwards to the depths—
whichever spatial metaphor we prefer) within ourselves, and
horizontally to its realisation in everyone else. It is the
unitive knowledge of God which, as we have several times
noted, is what salvation is all about. The test of its genuine-
ness, needless to say, is not in any feelings or emotions or
private visions, but in how realistically we recognise the
people we meet with day by day, not as individuals separated
off from us, but as one with ourselves. Inevitably we are
brought back to the divine commonplaces: the call to
compassion, patience, friendliness, helping those in need,
learning the humility which excludes anger, remembering
that we are all one, sharing the human condition together:
the forbearance we strive to show to others we are just as
much in need of ourselves. The poet's intuition may help us
to reach the heart of the Eucharist more rewardingly than
many a treatise in theology:

> And throughout all Eternity
> I forgive you, you forgive me.
> As our dear Redeemer said:
> 'This the Wine, and this the Bread.'[1]

[1] William Blake, *My Spectre around Me Night and Day*, xiv.

Appendix

The following article appeared in The Times *of London on 23 December 1972 under the editorial title 'A new star in the East for the institutional church'. It is here reproduced with the kind permission of the Editor.*

To have served recently for an agreeable month as Regents' Professor of Religious Studies at the University of California may excuse an ageing observer indulging in a series of personal comments on the state of religion today. The paradox of the whole situation was well formulated by the chairman of the religion department at the Riverside campus. 'We are faced all over America with an increasing interest in religion combined with a decreasing interest in the Church.'

For those who are persuaded by this view, yet hold that traditional Christianity still has a vital part to play in the spiritual destiny of the West, the matter is worth honest examination. Even such groups as the 'Jesus people' and the Pentecostalists—who see themselves as dedicated Christians with few leanings towards the Orient—apparently derive little active inspiration from the institutional Church. What has brought about this state of affairs? Is any change desirable? If so, in what direction? And how?

There can be little doubt that the scientific temper of the age, with its emphasis on control by evidence and the test of

experience, in contrast to religion's insistence on mystery and
blind faith, is a formidable challenge to any merely authoritarian presentation of Christian belief. Science has been well
described as 'a process of discovery rather than a compendium of data'. For many, this description could just as
easily apply to the personal religious quest. For the man in
the street, the search is not so much for revealed 'truth'
as for demonstrated meaning. Church renewal may well
remain a mirage until the Christian proclamation comes to
terms with these realities.

Few of today's younger generation have read William
James's *The Varieties of Religious Experience*, but the criteria
for valid religion which he laid down at the beginning of the
century are what in effect are now being sought. They are:
immediate luminousness, philosophical reasonableness and
moral helpfulness, to which we might go on to add the
element of aesthetic satisfaction. The ideal of the religious
person in the eyes of youthful, and not so youthful observers,
moving eastward from San Francisco, through New York to
London, has not been better expressed than it was by James
—'the disposition of the genuine child of God, the permanently patient heart, the love of self eradicated'.

As a variant of the paradox already noted we find that,
while a concern to bring together members of different
religions is widely discernible, interest in official ecumenism
has waned. The movement, to quote a prominent Epis-
copalian, has been rendered 'top heavy by the clergy'. A
great deal that makes for harmony and co-operation is
actually taking place, though well in advance of what has as
yet been juridically sanctioned. How to maintain and hand
on to the rising generation, and its successors, whatever is
true and of abiding value in the religion of the West, hitherto
formulated in traditional Christianity, might be considered
of greater urgency than finding the formula with which to
unite the Christian denominations.

From this standpoint the Church has nowhere to go but
inwards. At its present stage of development, there is hardly
anything more to be said about what a character in E. M.
Forster's *A Passage to India* described, somewhat unfairly, as
'poor little talkative Christianity'; all that remains is for it to
be properly understood and practised. The Church's routine
activities, the ministry of the word and the sacraments—
updated, for better or worse, as they have been—still leave
no lasting impact on large numbers of its own adherents.
The contemporary deviations into astrology, witchcraft and
various forms of occultism tell their own story. Most converts
to occultism, Father Richard Woods informs us in his recent
book *The Occult Revolution*, are Catholics who have abandoned
the Church because of its 'shallowness'.

Here also lies the explanation of the widespread turning
to the religions of the East, particularly the Hindu-Buddhist
tradition. In so far as this interest is consciously formulated,
the quest is not for the universalism of internationalists and
conventional liberals, but for something more native to the
average man and woman, 'the journey homeward to the
truest self'. Account must also be taken of the fact that many
of the younger generation are as conservative-minded as
their elders; they leave experimentation to the more ad-
venturous and are prepared to settle for what they hope are
their own roots, local, tribal, above all, personal.

But here again a paradox presents itself: the young people
who today remain unimpressed by the Church have probably never known the heart of it, being put off by its institutional framework; while those who are drawn to eastern
religions may have tasted their intoxicating spiritual essence,
but are unfamiliar with their own peculiar set of institutional
drawbacks.

Nevertheless, though western Christianity still has something to give to the East, it has probably more to gain from
the encounter. Such lessons as may be learned could come

more easily from quiet study and meditation rather than from verbal dialogue. In any religious discussion in India or South-East Asia, one is likely to be reminded of the aphorism of Lao Tzu: 'Those who know do not say; those who say do not know'; or this piece of Buddhist 'nonsense':

> The whole world is tormented by words
> And there is no one who does without words.
> But in so far as one is free from words
> Does one really understand words.

It must be admitted that the mental receptivity to be found in many parts of the United States probably provides a more favourable atmosphere for a meeting between Christianity and the Hindu-Buddhist tradition than what has recently been described as 'the stiflingly cosy cultural world of Britain'.

Yet it has been Englishmen, born or nationalised, combining metaphysical insight with notable literary gifts, rather than professional orientalists, who have absorbed and projected most effectively elements common to Catholic Christianity, the Vedanta and Mahayana Buddhism— Aldous Huxley, T. S. Eliot, and in his characteristically provocative way, Alan Watts. All three, however, clearly benefited from many years spent in the liberating climate of the United States. Huxley's interests were well known; he sacrificed his reputation as a novelist to a nobler cause. Eliot toyed for a time with Buddhism, describing the Buddha's Fire Sermon as 'corresponding in importance to the Sermon on the Mount'. The lines from *Little Gidding* reflect the Buddhist nirvana rather than Christian eschatology:

> This is the use of memory:
> For liberation—not less of love but expanding
> Of love beyond desire, and so liberation
> From the future as well as the past.

Watts, though unable to deny himself the role of gadfly, has brilliantly refuted the charge, still frequently made, either that the Hindu non-dualism is 'pantheistic', or the Buddhist doctrine of interdependently co-ordinated origination 'monistic'. He offers the salutary reminder that 'We are not to take our ego for God, but God for our ego.'

One point in particular where Indian religion has something to offer the West can easily be verified. Catholicism, following the Platonic and Aristotelian tradition, has divided human life between action and contemplation. Action, roughly speaking, is for those who live 'in the world', contemplation for those who live in solitude or enter monasteries or convents. This division has been elaborated with many ramifications and is by no means as simple as it looks: but it cannot compared in religious depth with the much subtler handling of the same theme in the *Bhavagad Gita* or in Patanjali's Yoga Sutras.

Yoga is associated in many western minds with breathing and bodily postures, which are only a minor part of it. Yoga means 'union', that is, a path to union with God. Broadly speaking, there are three such paths: the yoga of loving devotion to God; the yoga of selfless God-dedicated action; the yoga of meditation, whereby God is found by examining the real nature of phenomena. How pregnant, for example, are the words of the *Gita*: 'The world is imprisoned in its own activity, except when actions are performed as worship of God.' There is nothing un-Christian or specifically oriental about Yoga: Matthew 11.29, 30 reports Jesus as inviting his followers to adopt his own form of yoga (the Sanskrit word for 'yoke'); and it would be easy to show that his saving mission embodied many of the ideals of the Hindu and Buddhist sages.

The wellbeing of the Church may largely depend, not so much on solving contemporary questions of ecclesiology, as on reviewing its basic doctrines in the light of religious insights now being made available from the East. To take such a course would only be to revivify the spirit of the

Church's origins. New Testament scholarship indicates that the understanding of Jesus revealed in the Pauline epistles and the Fourth Gospel—itself the foundation of Christian theology—may owe not a little to Hellenistic, Iranian and possibly Buddhist sources. 'There is a real parallel between what Christian theologians call the understanding of the teaching of Christ in the light of the Easter event and the Mahayanist interpretation of the Buddha's doctrine.' So writes Father Edgar Bruns, offering 'new insights into the Fourth Gospel', in his recent monograph *The Christian Buddhism of St John.*

Here it is worth recalling that the first-century break between the New Israel and the Old—probably the greatest single tragedy, in itself and in its consequences, in the history of religion—was due to an over-anxious conservatism incapable of assimilating apparently alien doctrines. The loss to the Church would be incalculable if history repeated itself, and the arguments of those who prefer to remain 'safely walled in by historic creeds and codes' were to prevail. Christianity would have forfeited its title to be a truly world religion.

Let it be allowed that the indispensable role of the institutional Church is to be a conservative influence. The younger generation's attack upon 'structures' is a healthy challenge to churchmen to be mindful of their limitations, both official and personal; but 'doing one's own thing' could be as egotistically unspiritual as any exercise in ecclesiastical power politics. Traditionalism, ranging from the enlightened to the obscurantist, has been bound up with historic Christianity from its start. For this reason Church administrators can rarely be leaders of religious thought; their role is to be spokesmen and apologists for doctrinal positions to which they are officially committed.

What calls for greater recognition, however, is that the voice of authority is not necessarily the voice of truth, still less of understanding and compassion. In the last analysis, a religious standpoint must be self-authenticating. This is particularly true in the area of moral conduct, where any attempt to lay down general ethical principles must always be tempered by the proviso that circumstances alter cases. The ideal should be upheld before those to whom it applies, but as a goal to be aimed at rather than a mandatory burden indiscrimately imposed. From which it follows that the mood of wise Church government in today's world will be persuasive. In necessary truths let there be unity, wrote St Augustine in his day—though we are now rather less sure than he was about what these truths are. More pertinent to our situation are the concluding phrases of his maxim: 'In what is doubtful let there be liberty, but in all things let us have charity.'

More than half the population of the world, according to a United Nations survey, are now under twenty-four. What these young people want, says Arthur Blessitt in his readable and moving paperback *Turned on to Jesus*, is something beyond sacraments and liturgy or socially orientated Christianity; it is 'the essence of God, his relevance to their lives, his personal meaning to them'. Yet we learn from a questionnaire sent to American students that 80 per cent of the respondents expressed 'a need for religious faith', while only 48 per cent acknowledged any belief in God. Similarly in West Germany, 86 per cent admitted to praying, while only 68 per cent said they believed in God. These findings can perhaps be more easily reconciled in the light of what lies manifest in the Hindu-Buddhist tradition rather than in Christianity as popularly expounded.

Possibly the simplest way to discuss this problem is to raise the question whether the Church has not been too much concerned with religion *about* Jesus, too little with the religion *of* Jesus. In Mahayana Buddhism, for example, the faithful are encouraged to believe that the Buddha's luminous state of consciousness, what is held to be his supreme degree of wisdom and compassion, is open to everyone. This is the prospect which is attracting so many in the West to Buddhism today—to which must be added its apparent harmony with much that is disclosed in the sciences of physics and psychology. Referring to what is to be said about the origin of the world, Nigel Calder in his *Violent Universe* speaks of the latest astronomical discoveries as being 'bad for Moses but bully for the Buddha'.

Correspondingly, a question that can profitably preoccupy the minds of today's Christians is, in what degree the God-centred consciousness of Jesus is attainable by them. That this happens to be what Christianity is all about is rather more than hinted at in passages from both the Pauline epistles and the Fourth Gosepl. But the point may have been obscured by undue emphasis being placed on the activities of the ministerial priesthood, together with the Church's concern to maintain its own structures. Could it be that in striving to attain the Christ-consciousness, as here indicated, we have the only effective foundation for Christian renewal?

To achieve 'the mind of Christ' may well demand a profound re-thinking of Christianity's prayer life. Telling God, reverentially, what he should do, and people, indirectly, how they ought to behave, together make up a good deal of the Church's vocal prayers. They are hardly enough for those who believe themselves to be sharers in the divine nature, who wish to realise experientially such a state and make it known to others. Priests of the future, it may be, will learn not only to preside at the Eucharist but to lead the faithful in meditation, after the manner of an Eastern guru. For something more personality-enhancing than prayers of petition, or even praise, is required if genuine spiritual enlightenment and freedom are to be achieved.

Serious meditational practice, though there is much demand for it, is still a rarity in the western Church. Its doctrinal justification, however, has been latent in the Christian tradition from the beginning. The Hindu view that God is to be known as 'not this, not that' (*neti, neti*), the Buddhist teaching that the fulness of reality discloses itself to mental 'emptiness' (*shunyata*), are both to be found in the writings of Denis the Areopagite. Possibly part of their inspiration actually stems from India. At any rate, it continued in the Church through such writers as St Thomas Aquinas, the author of *The Cloud of Unknowing*, St John of the Cross, John of Ruysbroeck and Dom Augustine Baker.

Obviously, this detached yet bliss-bestowing spirituality is only a part of the Christian story. That it should be widely retold and acted upon, by way of correcting an imbalance, is all that is here being suggested. Theology, like Wittgenstein's philosophy, 'will signify what cannot be said, by presenting clearly what can be said'. Similarly, perhaps, the Church's problems may to some extent be solved, 'not by giving new information, but by arranging what we have always known'.

Index